Dr. Faith on Faith

THE REALITIES

DR. FAITH E. HARTIE

ISBN 978-1-0980-7060-1 (paperback)
ISBN 978-1-0980-7462-3 (hardcover)
ISBN 978-1-0980-7061-8 (digital)

Christian Faith Publishing, Inc.
832 Park Avenue
Meadville, PA 16335
www.christianfaithpublishing.com

Printed in the United States of America

I dedicate this book to my deceased husband of 47 years, Allen Leroy Hartie and our loving daughter, Sherrae' Louella Hartie. You two have forever changed my life. Thank You!

MYOC

My Faith

Your Faith

Our Faith

Changes Things

Believers in the MYOC spiritual realm render
themselves to a life of purpose.

Contents

Faith Rocks

My unyielding spiritual faith
Keeps me empowered and spiritually strong
Faith keeps me from engaging in a lot of sin
and keep me from doing wrong
It often creates human stressors
When unfortunately, we allow ourselves
To engage in challenging moments
Our spirits feel the pressure

Faith heightens our sense of purpose
It keeps some of us very calm
And even from committing
Many awful and unlawful wrongs

Faith showers us with strength,
Courage, hope, and unmitigated power
The faithful; who internalize hope and faith
Purposely blooming
As faithful flowers
Faith guides
Faith provides
Faith sustains
Faith rewards
Faith strengthens
Faith maintains
Faith Rocks!

Part 1

My Faith

Dr. Faith on Faith

Faith: What is it?

- Faith is often defined by most as: complete trust or confidence in someone or something (Google).
- Faith is also seen as a strong belief in God or in the doctrines of a religion based on spiritual perceptions discernment rather than proof (Google).

Definition and quotes

- Faith is the substance of things hoped for, the evidence of things not seen (Hebrews 11:1).
- "The greatest legacy one can pass on to one's children and grandchildren is not money or material things accumulated in one's life, but rather a legacy of character and faith" (Billy Graham).
- "We need to reject any politics that targets people because of their race or religion. This isn't a matter of popular correctness. It's a matter of understanding what makes us strong. The world respects us not just for our arsenal but; it respects us for our diversity and openness and the way we respect every faith" (Barack Obama).
- "Optimism is the faith that leads to achievement. Nothing can be done without hope and confidence" (Helen Keller).
- "Faith must be enforced by reasons…when Faith becomes blind it dies" (Mahatma Gandhi).
- "Be faithful in small things because it is in them that your strength begins" (Mother Teresa).

- "Faith is taking the first step even when you don't see the whole staircase" (Rev. Dr. Martin Luther King Jr.).
- "I believe if you keep your faith, you keep your trust, you keep the right attitude, if you're grateful, you'll see God" (Joel Osteen).
- "Keep your dreams alive. Understand to achieve anything requires Faith and belief in yourself, vision, hard work, determination, and dedication. Remember all things are possible for those who believe" (Gail Devers).
- "Faith is like a radar that sees through the fog" (Corrie ten Boom).
- "Life is full of happiness and tears, be strong and have faith" (Kareena Kapoor Khan).
- "Technology is nothing. What's important is that you have Faith in people, that they are basically good and smart, and if you give them the tools, they will do wonderful things with them" (Steve Jobs).
- "Faith is the bird that feels the light when the dawn is still dark" (Rabindranath Tagore).
- "Faith is the love taking the form of aspiration" (William Ellery Channing).
- "Always be yourself, express yourself, have faith in yourself, do not go out and look for a successful personality and duplicate it" (Bruce Lee)!
- "He took my hand and I graciously let go of my plans… faith" (Ellen Grimes).
- "And now abideth faith, hope, and charity, these three: but the greatest of these is charity" (1 Corinthians 13:13).

Faith on Faith Quotes

Faith E. Hartie

- Your faith is your invisible, spiritual power source, allowing you to eliminate obstacles and alter situations.
- Rock your faith every day and in every way, faith makes our world a better place to pray and to safely stay.
- Your faith works. So work your faith.
- Building your faith circle can be as challenging as building your family/friends circle, but just as rewarding.
- Let your faith light your way.
- As God's rain sprinkles and nourishes the earth and all that is within, let your faith continue to nourish you and all that you love.
- God gently reached down and touched our soul and our faith was spiritually ignited.
- May your glorious faith rainbow, given by God, spread the luster of colors made by God's intangible and radiant light:

Red: passion
Orange: creativity
Yellow: energy
Green: fertility
Blue: divinity
Indigo: self-awareness
Violet: high spiritual mastery

Which rainbow color represents your faith color today? Why?

- Spread your spiritual wings and make your true inner faith soar throughout the atmosphere and courageously impact positive change.
- Your fears are tiny little holes in your soul and will be filled with conviction, confidence and trust, if only you hold onto your faith, step back, and let God.

- Soul to soul and spirit to spirit, our faith prevails and keeps us inspirationally whole and purposeful.
- Stand strong in God's Word, your faith, and purpose for his power is almighty and all giving. Burdens we bear are the challenges of life we experience to strengthen our resolve. They broaden our scope of intense struggles and daily temptations. Faith provides management mechanisms and successfully guides through.
- In your loneliest and darkest hour call out "Almighty, grant me peace, solace, and solution." Stand strong on your faith in his glory and God's power.
- When you suffer from waning faith due to stressing situational issues, nourish your soul with the spiritual feedings of your Higher Power.
- Give God the praise and glory and *you* keep the faith. If you are true to your faith, you will give, give, and give of yourself at no cost. It's what God expects of his faithful.
- Use your unmitigated faith values to *stomp* out evil…good over evil…faith rules!
- Inner faith denotes your fundamental attitude, potential altitude, and aptitude to excel.
- Your faith evolves as beautifully as the plumes of our God's creatures, if we constantly nourish our hearts, souls, and minds with the words of the Almighty!
- Life's ups and downs are inevitable. Faith in God transcends all. We must believe in God's power! God can and will do all things, if only we trust and believe.
- No suicide! Choose to survive!
- God's got the power to make us thrive!
- Suicide is not an option, beleve that your faith in GOD and related assistance will show you new options.

Suicide Help Resources

Kristen Brooks Hope Center 800 Suicide (7842433)
The Veterans Crisis Line Trans Lifeline HopeLine

Georgia Crisis & Access Line
National Suicide Prevention Lifeline 800 273 Talk [8255]
Asian American Suicide Prevention & Education 8779908588
Boys Town Suicide and Crisis Line 800 448 3000 (text, chat, email)
Facebook:
https/www.facebook.com/crisistextline

A brand-new day
A brand-new opportunity
A brand new experience
Always
Make good use of your faith and time!

Faith, family, and friends
Make the world go round
Enjoy the journey

May our faith practices delete the current
Hate and racist tones!
Let there be peace and love!

Manage your faith
Manage your choices
Miracles will happen;
Just believe

Live your daily life with strong faith,
And planned purpose.
Talk the positive talk!
Walk the positive walk!

May our faith continuously evolve
And create an atmosphere of "hope," for those suffering today.
May our emotional, psychological, and physical pains be lifted.
Pray that our personal issues, worldly conflicts, and heartfelt
Challenges/loss be diminished.

1

What Is Faith to You?

My thoughts

I accept and ultimately agree that faith is an internal psychological, emotional, and spiritual manifestation of man's self-to-self beliefs. The self-to-self perspective versus the self-to-others is my personal view of man indulging in his faith practices within oneself, versus him dealing with the outside world of humanity.

Self-to-self indulgences involve one looking into oneself and owning the values, mores, beliefs, and tolerances that make *you you.* I frequently connect to Michael Jackson's song "Man in the Mirror" when alluding to the self-to-self experience. The fact that you and I are the sum total of our teachings, experiences, and our environment often explains numerous behaviorisms we demonstrate.

Within the self-to-self purview, mankind conducts introspection and acts accordingly with self as one's faith is involved in decision-making. As individuals we are constantly making choices dealing with how, what, with, whom, and why should self act or react to circumstances impacting our own lives.

How many times have you talked to yourself about stuff? You have had your own mental wrestling matches with personal matters that are weighing on you. These are your self-to-self moments. No one but your Higher Power and you know of the emotional conflict you're experiencing unless you choose to make it a self-to-others moment by informing others of your dilemma(s), thereby seeking external assistance in making the final decision(s) as to the course of action(s) to be taken.

Examples: self-to-self conflicts

- Should I go to work today?
- Can I climb the mountain? Should I climb it? Why? Why not?
- Should I invest in these stocks?
- Which bill should I pay this month?
- What college/university is most apt to fulfill my needs?
- Is this relationship worthy?
- Should I take out a loan for additional schooling? New car? House?
- Should I commit to a religious sect?
- Should I cut, color, braid my hair?

The self-to-others concept is purely applied to the engagement of one's faith when interacting or in the consideration of all others. We are often perplexed by our global observations of our human counterparts. Wars, political coos, traditional practices (domestic, cultural, economic) are inadvertently found to be problematic for various societies.

We observe daily human faith-based interactions reflecting how, we, as the most evolved living creature, on the earth maintain our own personal sanity, dignity, and humanity throughout time. Our beliefs, trust, confidence, assurances, and convictions, along with the human observations, create self-to-self and self-to-others transformations.

Mentally and emotionally I perceive the self-to-others concept as the most daunting engagement because it is so personal. It determines how an individual behaves, aspires to induce positive relationships, as well as enhance personal growth and overall development.

The self-to-others concept relates to the idea of an individual's faith and its global connect. The world's aura is fundamentally tuned into the behaviors of mankind. Neighborhoods, cities, states, countries, and continents are constructed for and by people. The faith-based decisions and institutions governing the entities determine the social, economic conditions, and political status. People of like-minded faith tend to manage in similar patterns.

From a global perspective mankind tends to interact in a plethora of ways that project our faith. We often engage in the following activities:

o   Treat and mistreat
o   Understand and misunderstand
o   Engage and disengage
o   Encourage and discourage
o   Create life and destroy life
o   Heal and maim
o   Organize and disorganize
o   Respect and disrespect
o   Accept and reject
o   Employ and deploy
o   Love and hate

We proceed on life's journey, maintaining that faith guides us through. This journey has exposed me to a number of moments when I've questioned God, but not my faith in God. For example, failure, loss of loved ones, challenge experiences naturally create in many of us the "why" feelings.

As a person, like many people, I've been in situations where I've felt some disrespect. It had its effects, good and bad. Each incident provided life lessons that overtime help me develop major coping mechanisms. I am sharing two examples, race oriented. First, in the 1960s my mother and I would often go into center city on Saturdays. This day we were in Wanamaker's department store, we were waiting at the jewelry counter, waiting for service. Five minutes, ten minutes passed by, no one came over to us while we watched others being acknowledged and serviced.

Patience had reached a boiling point, and we questioned the Caucasian saleslady, who was quite nonchalant about the situation. In a rather arrogant manner she asked what did we want. Unfortunately, our faith was tested that day. We both failed. Out of anger we said some things that were not Christian-like and moved on, without making a purchase.

Unbelievably so, about fifty years later, I went to Bayside, in Miami, Florida, in 2009. I went into a little handbag and shoe boutique, my daughter and I were browsing. We had looked around for about five minutes, and she never asked if she could help us. The salesperson ignored us and went to the next woman that entered; of course she and the other woman were of the same ethnicity. My daughter, who lived in Florida, about five years before this happened, informed me that some, not most, Latinos have a less than positive image of African Americans, in many cases due to social media and the news.

Both situations reflected a certain attitude some people have toward others different from themselves. We all have some prejudices and biases. They are not always race related. I have learned to accept people and judge them on their own merit and treat them accordingly. Generalizations made about various groups of people, with a connectedness to skin color, language, or religious affiliations unfortunately is common. It can be detrimental to relationships and societal progress. Our global society still has to willingly and completely engage in the change process. It is a formidable challenge, but my faith facilitates favorable transformations.

Thought

Developing, cultivating, and refining relationships is a primary focus of my faith. My faith stimulates and motivates me as I transport myself from one situation to another. My faith directs my conversation, psychological, and physical interactions with the universe as life challenges me.

My faith is my inner spiritual trust and belief in God and mankind. It is my daily dose of righteousness.

> For in the gospel the righteousness of God
> is revealed a righteousness that is by Faith by first
> to last just as it is written: The righteous shall live
> by faithfulness. (Romans 1:17)

2

What Are Your Four Strong Areas of Faith?

The first area I consider a strength is my trust in God and his Word. Trust is the primary facet of my faith. The fact that I trust God to guide me through my life's journey is a comforter. I am blessed to be given the brainpower to indulge in creative thinking, problem-solving, and emotional decision-making. From experience, I know and trust God to put human angels in my path when most needed. My life is often complicated, frequently requiring me to trust in the Lord and "keep it moving."

Confidence is my second area of strength. I have strong confidence in my faith. Life consistently provokes situations that implore the use of self-confidence. Seeking employment or promotions, high academic achievements, extraordinary athletic accomplishments, successful relationships demand more displays of high levels of confidence. Faith in oneself is key to reaching pinnacles in life.

My faith has developed in me, an attitude of "I can do!" Throughout my life I have taken risks with personal visions. There are three that stand out:

- *Faith Hartie's Model's 8 INC.* This was the modeling agency that I originated in the mid-1970s. It was functional until 1980. I coordinated fashion shows throughout the tristate area and worked as an agent for print and runway models.

- *Tutorial Technology Arts Project (TuTech).* This was an educational extracurricular project which I developed and received federal funding to conduct at the Riletta Twyne Cream Family School in Camden, New Jersey. Dorothy Womble Wyatt was the school Principal and and progressive leader. Students and some grandparents participated in the Saturday morning program. The program began in the mid-1990s and was available to the school community for approximately five years.

- *Small Learning Communities (SLCs) at the Woodrow Wilson High School, under the Principalship of Calvin Gunning in Camden, New Jersey.* I developed three stages of implementation for the SLC program. I also supervised a team of teachers and administrators, who transitioned the educational paradigm from the traditional model to Small Learning Communities. The idea was to provide students with educational choices based on career interests. I also worked with a professional grant writer and a few fellow colleagues. We received SLC grants for the two comprehensive high schools, in the amount of $88,000.00 each. Each school spent the grant money to transform the schools, improve instruction, and elevate test results.

Each one of these endeavors presented its own set of challenges before and during the implementation processes. My confidence, persistence, and determination were three of the foundations these programs warranted to succeed and provide the much-needed services. Once again, my faith was sufficient.

Conviction is my third strongest facet of my faith. Internalizing conviction, as it applies to phases of my life, supplies me with the certitude and strength needed to meet the daily challenges, goals, and aspirations. My strong conviction builds my constitution as a person of purpose.

Finally, I acknowledge my spiritual ideology as my fourth strongest area of faith. Living by the spiritual doctrines of my faith perpetuates the religious practices I grew to embrace during my childhood and throughout my lifetime.

Thought

In conclusion, trust in God, confidence, conviction, and my spiritual ideology are the four strongest aspects of my faith. I firmly believe, "If you don't stand for something, you'll fall for anything." I stand for faith.

3

What Is One Area of Faith You May Need to Strengthen? Ideology

Ideology

1. visionary theorizing; a systematic body of concepts especially about human life or culture (*Merriam Webster*).
2. The body of doctrine, myth, belief, etc. that guides an individual, social movement, institution, class, or large group (www.dictionary.com).

Increasing my knowledge of God's Word, the comprehension of the ideology of the Gospel, is needed to elevate my faith. Bible teachings are a priority to heighten my understanding of life and mankind. The Holy Bible contains wisdom and empowerment, embedded in stories and verses.

My exposure to the Holy Bible and its lessons has occurred since my early childhood. Sunday school, Bible study, and sermons have provided me with a spiritual foundation that is rooted in my soul. But I am absolutely thirsty for greater understanding of the Gospels. I need to enhance my use of God's Word through my thoughts, words, and deeds.

A few ideologies, I incorporate into my daily psyche, I fondly call my faithisms:

- Do unto others as you would have them do unto you.
- Maintain an attitude of gratitude.
- Teamwork makes the dream work.
- Talk the talk and walk the walk.
- Lead by example.
- Dare to care.
- Create and maintain a nontoxic environment.
- Develop a strong collaborative culture.
- Reach out and touch.
- Each one teach one.
- God guides and God provides.
- God is the Alpha and Omega.
- Walk by faith and not by sight.
- Faith transforms.
- Faith renews.
- Faith motivates and stimulates.
- Faith promotes positivity
- Faith transcends.
- Faith prevails.
- Faith grants charity.
- Faith grants hope.

Thought

I sincerely realize that my faith is my soul's daily supplement to improved behaviors, increased trust, and understanding. The ideologies that I have and will continue to internalize assist me in achieving the higher level of faithfulness.

4

Do You Think the American Society is Faith Based?

Faith-based (FBOs) organizations, research networks, health services research, health promotion, places of worship or congregations represent not only physical safe spaces, but also extensive reach into neighborhoods through complex social networks. FBOs provide organized access to resources, such as trust, health care, informal support, job and educational opportunities.

(Google Dictionary) Article abstract: FaithBased organizations Science and the Pursuit of Health Globally From the beginning of time, societies have engaged in practicing their faiths. Churches, cathedrals, synagogues, temples, and mosques are the traditional buildings used to recruit and educate the masses. Within these walls the leaders, expand the spiritual worship circles and elevate the levels of faith. The worship ideologies, philosophies, spiritual concepts, convictions, and strong beliefs engineer the human behaviors of the specified followers. Faith-based activities have evolved from these spiritual groups and cultures. Traditionally these activities originate from the four major human needs: hunger, shelter, thirst, and love.

Society has given titles to their specific deities; God, Jehovah, Allah, Abba, Yahweh, Lord, the Light, and the Creator. The followers of the various worship centers usually support faith-based programming.

Man has created programs that aid and assist their fellow humans that are challenged in some manner. Economical, spiritual, emotional, psychological, or sociological issues have faith-based program developed around them. Improving and maintaining the integrity and success of these programs is dependent upon the trust and conviction of the leaders and the participants. The following programs are examples of faith-based organizations:

- Drug and Alcohol Rehab-Addiction Treatment Center
- Medi-Shared Christian Healthcare
- Give a Bible, Change a Life Open Door USA
- Catholic Charities
- Habitat for Humanity
- Salvation Army
- ADRA Adventist Disaster Relief Agency
- Alliance to end Hunger
- Global Health Ministries
- Feed the Children
- Mission Without Borders World Hope International
- DREAMS (Determined, Resilient, Empowered, Aids free, Mentored & Safe women)

Thought:

The world is a better place because of the existence of faith-based organizations. The fact that their universal FBO programs provide much needed services to the less fortunate is key to the concept of FBOs.

5

How Can Your Faith Impact Personal Situations?

Faith impacts every aspect of my life, in one situation or another. I perpetuate this concept: MYOC (My Faith, Your Faith, Our Faith, Changes Things). It fundamentally creates the aura of expectations. Inclusivity is my spirit of choice. Transforming the world into a better planet, less war, more peace (globally, personally, economically, and politically) are one of my daily visions. "If everyone lit just one little candle, what a bright world this would be" is a familiar quote with a dynamic message and an even greater challenge to mankind.

My faith determines behavioral jesters and emotional displays of kindness, generosity, and caring toward most situations involving others. Giving people the benefit of the doubt is also in my wheelhouse. Apprehension levels are not very high as I approach new relationships and situations. Situational circumstances often require the implementation of invasive and pervasive strategies for resolution. Trust, conviction, and ideologies are faith derivatives that impact personal situations. Job-related situations are definitely impacted by one's faith. I have been gainfully employed since I was fourteen years old. I started in recreation (ten years) and worked in education (forty-two years) with a couple of sidelines. Fortunately, I have had a series of overall successful job experiences. It was not always easy to maintain my sanity, but my faith adequately prevailed.

Inevitably challenging situations arise wherever you work or socialize. Each situation comes with its own unique set of conditions and opportunities or lack thereof, depending upon to whom you are responsible. Also job security is determined by how skillful you are in meeting your obligations. Your faith usually dictates your ability to comply and successfully maneuver throughout the given situation.

Thought

Each day I awake, look in mirror, and see me. The self-to-self introspection occurs. I contemplate how to make situations better for all concerned. Human err does happen; sometimes I make horrendous choices that come with regrets and often despair. But I continue to embrace my faith and my beliefs that have served me well in the past. So I pray:

> I will lift up mine eyes to the hills, from hence cometh my help. My help cometh from the Lord, which made heaven and earth. He will not suffer thy foot to be moved: he that keepeth thee will not slumber. (Psalm 121:13)

6

Do You Have Faith? In What?

Life is what it is because of the faith that has been instilled in me from the cradle-up. Living my spiritual beliefs often presents its challenges due to both positive and negative personal habits. I am a Christian in training. I have faith in God's power. I know the power of the Lord for I have seen the wonders of his glorious work. Faith in mankind and myself are variables I use to further manage life's challenges. My faith continues to be reinforced by the multitude of visible blessings.

My imperfections are works in progress. Assuring myself that if I continue to strive for near excellence I'll at least experience a degree or two of positive growth in those specified areas. It is my aspiration to live a life of faithfulness that may inspire, motivate, and encourage others.

Motivation to practice my faith comes from God and trusting in his words. Stepping out on faith is one affirmation I live by each day. Another affirmation is faith can and does move mountains. A number of major life's decisions have been determined by my convictions, beliefs, and purpose.

I possess a certain propensity, allowing me to recognize elements of faith in my fellow man, and it usually results in predictable and appropriate experiences. Faith in certain people is natural. Relationships are built of faith and trust. My best, best girlfriend (BBFF) since I was eight years old, is Delores Davis (Dee). We have been through thick and real thin times. Our faith has been challenged many times, through death, disappointments, pain, and tribulations, but still, "We Rise!" However, like most, I've made some mistakes in faith placement. I've had my fair share of disappointments.

As a global society, from coast to coast and continent to continent, we are traditionally a blend of attitudes, aptitudes, values, mores, and philosophical views. The variations and differences inadvertently create some misunderstandings and misjudgments. Often, we find ourselves marred in conflicts that result in societal disruption, chaos, confusion, and fatalities.

MYOC is a catalyst for improving some of the mayhem that is consciously or unconsciously initiated by man. Faith is the resolution of misunderstandings, differences, religious conflicts, and political platform unrest. Collaborative actions involving trust and conviction are powerful tools to improving negatives situations. Only if and when man is amenable to transcend the variables and differences for the greater good will we as a global society advance from a humanistic perspective.

Faith in the Almighty has granted me a multitude of blessings. I will gladly share some with you, and hopefully you will relate to my strong reliance on faith:

- Forty-seven years of marriage
- Birth of our baby girl Sherrae' Luella Hartie (after five years of struggle, a miscarriage, fertility issues)
- Twenty-one-year classroom teacher, writing teacher, mentor teacher
- Teacher of the year 198?
- Eleven years educational curriculum supervisor
- One year middle school principal
- Two years director of secondary curriculum and instruction
- Tutorial Technology Arts Project
- MASE Tech
- Model's 8 Inc.
- Eight years director of Christian Education (church)
- Faith Talk /MYOC Series (on Facebook)

Most of these blessings came with challenges that required my faith in God to get me through. A quote that means so much to me, as I reflect on my blessings is "Every journey begins with a little Faith" (author unknown).

I've known since I was five years old that Jesus really loves me. My faith was tested and assured one evening when my father was returning my little two-year-old brother and me to my mother, awaiting our return. My parents were separated, and my father had picked us up earlier for a day outing. It was late evening as we rode the subway home. He carried my sleeping brother and held my hand as we stood near the doors in the crowded train. Several stops occurred and the next stop was quickly approaching when riders moved hurriedly to the opening door, brushing against us. My hand suddenly was torn from my father's. I found myself outside on the crowded train platform. As people quickly made their exit from the subway station, I realized my father and brother Frank were gone. They were still on the train. I ran down the platform crying and calling, "Daddy." Several people cornered me to ask questions.

Finally, this one man took my hand and said, "Come with me. We will get you home." I was so frightened and flustered by the whole three- to five-minute train and platform catastrophe, I willingly went with him—a stranger. He took me to a place (don't remember where), he asked for my address. He called the police, and they came and took me to 2035 Norris St. I looked out at the houses and said, "That's not my house." They had misunderstood. I told them again, "2035 North St." I guess some missing front teeth may have been the culprit. Needless to say, everyone was so relieved and happy to see me safe and sound. My father was in the doghouse for years. Future outings were abolished.

As I grew older, I mentally revisited the subway incident over and over again throughout time. The stranger became the "angel in my path." His act of kindness saved me from possible horrors, possibly rendering me emotionally disabled, physically harmed, or dead. My faith in God and mankind was forever increased. The stranger will forever have a special place in my heart. I regret I will never be able to inform him of the importance of his actions that evening. The caring stranger is one of my forever angels.

Thought

Faith in the Almighty is unequivocally substantiated by the existence of the earthly (humans, animals, plants, tree, foul) and heavenly bodies (Sun, Moon, stars, planets, etc.,) oceans, and all that constitutes the motion and flow of the entire universe. God's power is the single source of the atmosphere, troposphere, stratosphere, mesosphere, thermosphere, and exosphere. *His* majesty alone created and maintains the world as we know it and beyond. Faith in him is the construct of all that exists. Mankind attempts to successfully sustain and enhance a minuscule part of it all.

The faith in the Higher Power is all purposeful and all giving.

It is my utmost belief that my faith in the Omnipotent is justifiable; he is the only creator that could have supplied the universe with all that has been previously mentioned. Knowing that he did, I know he has the power to do anything and everything.

I am the Way, and the Truth, and the Life. (John 14:6)

All our dreams can come true if we have the courage to pursue them. (*Rediscover Jesus*, Matthew Kelly, 36)

Be strong and courageous, and act!
Do not fear nor be dismayed,
For the Lord God my God is with you.
(1 Chronicles 28:20 NASB)

7

Does Your Faith Give You an Extraordinary Sense of Power and/or Peace?

Reflecting on key possible fatalistic moments in my life, including near car accidents, emits a definitive poignancy. I claim the empowerment and moments of peace provided by my faith during these moment and remembrances. I name it, claim it, and frame the notion that my faith enhances my power to endure and sustain life in the manner in which God directs. Peace in the daily course of living is an asset. It automatically increases chances to efficiently handle business with confidence and resolve. God's power rules my world. I give God the glory and praise for the blessings. The God-given gifts, love, peace, confidence, and the inner power instilled in me are priceless.

Ordinarily, we don't get to select our families or gender, which are a nucleus of our lives. My blended Webb/Adamson/Hartie family has absolutely impacted and influenced my faith. Their love, spiritual guidance, encouragement, and confidence in me have fundamentally structured my faith-based approach to my reality.

A few incidences have occurred in my life that depict how my faith has given me the power to achieve and maintain a sense peace:

- The driving license saga. I was twenty-two years old when I got married. I didn't have a car or a license. I realized that I needed both. Rule of thumb, license first, then car. Well,

I sent for my permit and started taking formal driving lessons. My husband also taught me and let me practice in his car. Test time came, I failed the driving portion. Two weeks later, I went again and failed again. Two weeks later I went again, and finally I passed. Three trips to the DMV in order to be a licensed driver.

None of my family or friends had that challenging experience. I felt the disdain of failure each time, but my internal power was relentless. I was going to obtain that license by "any means necessary." My nerves kept getting in my way, but my faith prevailed. There was peace after the success. I felt a strong sense of power and peace.

■ After eight years of emotional, physical, and mental anguish and struggle, I recently lost my husband of forty-seven years to Parkinson's disease compounded with Alzheimer's, congested heart failure, and chronic kidney disease. Unfortunately, most of his doctors found his declining condition to be extremely fragile, two years prior to his passing. God had blessed me to be available to keep him home during the eight-year stretch, which was accompanied with frequent hospitalizations. My daughter, Sherrae', family members, and visiting nurse programs provided the much-needed in-home support. It was an extremely difficult time in our lives, but my husband was so worthy of our personal care. I am forever thankful to God and all the individuals that God sent to help us in our home. The African quote "It takes a village" is the epitome of how we felt, as family, friends, and caregivers faithfully attended to our needs.

I was often advised it would be better for me to put him in an aging facility. My faith in God and mankind made me say, "That was not an option." My faith in the Lord is all powerful, and I found immense peace in that thought.

Thought

For in the gospel the righteousness of God
is revealed a righteousness that is by Faith from
first to last just as it is written: the righteous shall
live by Faith. (Romans 1:17)

8

Has Your Faith Ever Been Broken?

After examining my three scores and then committing to a period of introspection, I can sincerely announce, my faith has never been totally broken. My faith has provided me with the spiritual power to overcome most of my life's struggles. I don't recall, even during my most discouraging moments, any deep feelings of hopelessness. My faith always strengthened my resolve. The confidence, physical and psychological strength, and spiritual guidance gifted to me through God's grace and mercy have lifted me out of the trouble zone a multitude of times. I am so grateful for the numbers of blessings my faith has awarded me.

Over the seventy years, I've cried, broken out with rashes, had sleepless nights, and sent up thousands of prayers, calling out, "God, Father Almighty, help me!" Never in my life have I felt God's absence, hence the power of my faith has forever reigned. We've all experienced highs and lows, peaks and valleys, victories and defeats. That's life, but faith determines how we react. This thought relates to popular expression "Life is 10% of what happens and 90% is how we respond to it."

Sharing a few of my life's perilous moments that rocked and confirmed my faith:

- A college experience enlightened me even more as to the majesty of God and the purpose of one's faith. Upon returning home from a cabaret, a college girlfriend and I disembarked a public bus at three in the morning, conversing with each other about the great fun we had that evening. We stepped off the bus, a few blocks from my home. As we started to move toward the curb, a man stepped out of the shadow with a gun in hand. He told us to give him our pocketbooks. We were frozen in time. We dropped our pocketbooks. He grabbed them and ran. Thank you, Lord. He left us physically unharmed. Mentally we were devastated.

We were stunned, having stared down the barrel of a gun. Our hearts were pounding. With weak knees, we quickly ran home. Out of fear and desperation we never told anyone. I was scared, feeling near-death experience, and I'm very embarrassed and hurt that my close friend had to experience such horror in my lower economic community. I never envisioned such a thing ever happening.

You are probably wondering why I didn't involve the police.

The thief had our ID and knew where I lived. My friend lived far away from my neighborhood. She lived on campus, and her home was in another state. Plus my parents probably would never, ever again let me travel at night. That would mean no more cabarets or parties, and maybe even dates. In the future, I took excessive safety measures when out late, and in all truth, all of the time.

■ A car situation also had brought about some intense moments that could have resulted in a major personal injury and a crushed Mercedes. Stopping at one of my school sites for a supervisory visitation, I accidentally ran the rear end of my vehicle over a curb in the winding driveway. The rear end passenger wheel of the car hung about four to five feet above the ground below. It was approximately a three-to-four-foot drop. I didn't realize the positioning of the rear when I tried to drive forward. When I couldn't get the car to move forward, I tried to move backward. Thanks to God's mercy, it still didn't move. I got out and walked to the back. I was aghast. I looked down at the ground below and the back wheel and thought, "Thank you, Lord, for not letting it drop off the curb."

I went into the school building and requested help. Custodians came out and tried a couple things; they realized it was too dangerous to continue. They had to call someone with a tow truck. He was able to save my Benz from a brutal crash. I was so thankful to all who helped resolve this hair-raising situation.

Thoughts

Our faith can and will be challenged in life. Restoring my faith has not been a major issue for me. Every day God replenishes it through his mercies, beginning with my daily awakening.

The trust you possess in your Higher Power provides you with the resolve and resilience to face and overcome your challenges. God had embraced me, as always, and, once again, brought me back from the brink of near tragedy. One more pump to the pedal and car may have fallen to the lower level ground area with me in it. The belief in God's power and the power of your faith will bring you through. A verse I feel is relative:

> For it is with your heart that you believed and are justified, and it is with your mouth that you profess your faith and are saved. (Romans 10:10)

9

Has Your Faith Ever Needed Restoration?

Philosophically, it is noted that our lives are often complicated with unexpected challenges: illnesses, death, financial issues, relationship problems, political crisis, and numbers of others. They have jarred and shaken our faith, at one time or another. People naturally look to their "Higher Power" for solutions and/or answers. Much of the consternation experienced due to crisis situations wreak havoc in our lives. This often results in our calling on God to render our next steps.

Often the results of the Jesus's call are palatable and positive. On the other hand, there are those situations that challenge faith because they persist, create negativity, and often pain or fear. Frustration, agitation, and disappointment are the general results. During these saddening moments, people may begin to question their faith.

God the Holy Father embraces and comforts his imperfect children until he deems it appropriate to provide the solutions needed to satisfy their problematic circumstances. They often respond by saying, "Thank you, Jesus."

I have had my moments of "Why me?" But over the seventy years of living in this world, I've learned to accept, "Why not me?" God's blessings have been bountiful; who am I to question his will? I've learned to believe, as my mom and grandma used to say, "Take the bitter with the sweet, and the good with the bad."

If your faith is weakened during a trying episode, God provides you with opportunities to rebuild your faith, if you are a believer in God's power. The restoration of your faith will inevitably occur, if only your spiritual self is continuously fed with the Gospel.

As life would have it, while in college, I commuted during my freshman year. A male student transported me and another female student home from school each day. This particular day, we were riding along about a mile out from the college, and I noticed the car was swerving down the winding country road. In seconds the car, a Beetle Bug, ran up an embankment and flipped over onto the rag top of their vehicle. We were upside down. Moaning and groaning we tried to crawl out. Two of us freed ourselves and assisted the driver in getting out. The police arrived and wrote up the report, asked if we needed to go to the hospital. We all, by the grace of God, were only a little bruised and scratched up. So we decided not to go immediately to the hospital. I don't recall who took us home. But God knows we were happy to get there and be alive to talk about the survival of it all. It was later revealed that the male driver was under the influence. Well I shared the car incident with my parents and was taken to the doctor's office to be checked. I was X-rayed and no broken bones were found. My neck and back were a little stiff. So I went to therapy for six weeks. Once again, God took me to it, and he brought me through it. My faith was challenged; and my faith, once again, prevailed. I never lost faith; I never felt I needed it to be restored.

Thought

A cat with nine lives describes how I often see myself. My faith has continuously offset so much trauma and drama that could have forever changed my life. Because of God's favor, I can share the wonders of his work. I truly relate to these verses:

> And they that know thy name will put thy
> trust in thee, for thou, Lord, has not forsaken
> them, that seek thee. (Psalm 9:6)

My job is to take of the possible and trust God with the impossible. (Psalm 9:10)

Fear you not, for I am with thee. (Isaiah 41:10)

10

Does Your Faith Direct Your Daily Behaviors?

Every morning, through God's grace and mercy, I rise, open my eyes and see, I sit upright, my feet hit the floor running. Only my God's favor allows this moment. I say, "Thank you, Lord, for another new day!"

My sincerest belief is that my faith absolutely directs most of the steps I take each day. The majority of us have at least two aspects of daily living where we continuously infuse elements of our faith. The moments are domestic/family and professional/employment.

The spiritual inner sanctum of oneself normally affects our external exhibition of treatments toward others and reactions to situations. My first example is related to a professional experience:

As an eight-year-old, I knew education was my chosen profession. I always loved school, most of my teachers, and even liked most subjects. I held teachers in high esteem and desired to imitate them and aspired to be one.

Several times, as a child, I requested and got a chalkboard, pencils, and notebooks for Christmas. I would pretend to be a teacher, using my siblings and neighborhood friends as the students. My family and my faith guided me on the extensive journey to become an educator. I was the first in my immediate family to attend college and graduate. I served in the field of education for forty-two years. It was an amazing time in my life.

My faith and my parents, together, successfully directed my daily steps through a series of educational institutions, degrees, certifications, and positions.

The concept of "Paying it forward" has recently become a very popular phrase and universal civic action. Many of us, of like minds and spirituality, have practiced this idea for most of our lives. Globally, there are those who conscientiously perform acts of giving back via sharing blessings, mentoring, along with encouraging and empowering others to elevate their situations to acceptable or exceptional status. This self to others behavior designates the individual reacting to the needs of all others. Your faith dictates what, how, and when you engage in these acts of humanity.

Personally, I have followed my faith and served as a camp counselor, teacher, mentor to teachers, mentor to young ladies aspiring to be models, committee member of fundraising/charitable organizations sponsoring student scholarships. All my life, I've served in the church through choirs, usher boards, officer in Credit Union, missionary, steward, and trustee. Serving as the director of Christian education was among the most fulfilling. The years of service was driven by my faith. Helping each day, all others within my reach, is me "paying it forward."

The next experience I'm sharing is more domestic/family oriented:

I met my husband, Allen Leroy Hartie, in 1969. We married in 1970. We stayed married until his passing, January 28, 2018. For over forty-seven years we led a relatively good life. We had our highs and lows, which required both of us to be trusting and believe in the process of living life together. Only by the grace of God and our love did we maintain the union. Not so easy, as is documented by the number of divorces.

After about five years, we decided we wanted a child. Unlike many people, the act of becoming pregnant was not a "walk in the park." We had to seek fertility counseling, take tests, and pray our faith was strong enough to help us successfully procreate. Well, as life would have, I did get pregnant, but after five and a half months,

I prematurely delivered, June 10, 1978, a 14 oz. baby girl, Monique. Due to an underdeveloped respiratory system, she died on day 2. It was very disheartening and deflating. It was one of the most difficult moments of my life, and I experienced a great sense of failure. My faith endured. We got through it and were blessed to experience pregnancy again and successfully gave birth to our daughter, Sherrae', at 4:19 p.m. on December 16,1979. But not without issues. She was expected to be born February 3, 1980; she was a preemie. Birth weight was 3 lbs. 16 oz. So of course she was placed in an incubator. I had a fever after giving birth to her, and they wouldn't bring her to me for fear she might contract something. After twenty-one days, they released Sherrae' to come home. She was my birthday gift, January she came home. My birthday is January 12th. My faith had been shaken, but it moved mountains for us. Every day my faith rules and guides my steps.

Thought

My faith constantly directs my steps through the thick and thin of life. Journeys involve commitment, conviction, disappointment, and trust in the process. It enables me to maintain much-needed strength and mental endurance to put in the time and do the necessary work to make new realties!

> Jesus is a friend who walks in when the world has walked out. (*God's Little Devotional Book for Women*, 188)

> The things I have spoken unto you, that in me ye might have peace. In the world ye shall have tribulations: but be of good cheer, I have overcome the world. (John 16:33)

11

Do You Consider Yourself a Faithful Servant? Why or Why Not?

I am a work in progress as to trying to be a faithful servant. Filtering my genuine love, charity, peace, and humility into the atmosphere is my daily mantra. Perpetuating positive behaviors is promoted throughout the Bible, beginning with "love thy neighbor as thyself." This effort is generally embraced by the universe, according to respective religions.

Much to my chagrin, we are all imperfect beings and fall short of the mark of adequately handling relationship issues and situational matters.

So the numerous situational conflicts existing in today's world are not surprising. Striving to be a faithful servant entails the demonstration of near exemplary behaviors that your Higher Power will acknowledge as worthy.

Truthfully, I would love to love all people, but unfortunately some individuals do not want to comply with the Golden Rule: "Do unto others as you would have them do unto you" (Luke 6:31 KJV; Dictionary.com). A command based on the words of Jesus in the Sermon on the Mount: "All things whatsoever ye would that men should do to you, ye even so to them" (Matthew 7:12). The Mosaic law contains parallel commandment: "Whatever is hurtful to you, do not do to any other person."

The torment, hostility, and pure unadulterated evil that some humans subject their fellowman/woman/children to is inexplicable. Self-to-others relationships are forever damaged when the malicious behavior of those cruel and psychotic beings concentrate their ferocity upon the universe.

Horrific conditions, situations, and fatalities caused by these individuals inadvertently challenge some of my internal faith teachings. As I delve wholeheartedly into my self-to-self realm, I attempt to maintain a high level of faith in humanity and seek comprehension as to the purpose of the evil and the perpetrators.

My endeavor to be a faithful servant is ongoing. There are things that happen in life that are difficult to unhear or unsee that make doing all the righteous things very challenging and difficult. Consequently, all I can do is try to accomplish those deeds toward my fellow person(s) that demonstrate my spiritual faith.

Another pair of verses that are inevitably internalized and practiced by a faithful servant are:

> Thou shalt love the Lord thy God with all thy heart, and with all thy soul, and with all thy mind, and with all thy strength. (Mark 12:30)

This is the First Commandment.

> And the second is like namely this: Thou shall love thy neighbor as thyself. (Mark 12:31)

There is none other commandment greater than these!

Thought

My daily plight is to spread words of spiritual value and participate in situations that enhance the importance of faith and its empowerment, benefits, and purpose. My personal challenge is creating an aura of faith that God will recognize as an effort to be a blessing to someone and a forever faithful servant.

You can
accomplish more
In one hour with God
Than one lifetime
Without Him.
(*God's Devotional Book for Women*, 80)

Walk in wisdom...redeeming the time.
(Colossians 4:5)

12

Do Your External Behaviors Compliment and Confirm Your Internal Beliefs?

Character analysis undoubtedly entails a serious self-to-self moment. Do you practice what you preach? What do your actions tell God? What does your behavior emulate? What is your self-perception, and how do others perceive you?

If you can honestly respond, you may have a greater awareness of what aspects of your faith are being inculcated into your daily living. You will realize where improvement is warranted.

Personally, it is my sentiment that my external behaviors are considerably consistent in several ways. I strive to display a strong sense of positivity, caring, trustworthiness, and belief in the Holy Word. It is with my spiritual compass that I attempt to successfully maneuver through life's caverns. Be clear, I am not always on point when it comes to being a child of God. Misbehaviors manifest themselves within me, from time to time. However, I am putting forth my best efforts to improve.

As I often dialogue with myself, during my self-to-self moments, my faith dictates the decisions I make about my actions and interactions. My various attitudes and mood fluctuations impact my actions taken and my reactions displayed. My internal and spiritual principles of behavior are generally aligned with my external behaviors, according to some who know me.

A few examples of "reads" I've gotten over time:

At work one morning, a fellow coworker waited for me to complete signing in. She casually looked at me and said, "You can't really be happy every morning." I was surprised and somewhat loss for words. The lady continued, saying, "You always seem like you have no problems."

I smiled at her and thought about my reply. Within seconds I said, "Truth be told, no way. But thanks."

I later wondered what truly prompted her question. After some pondering, I thought it must be God working within me. First of all, I am *not* a morning person (wish I were). Many mornings, I wake up with numerous unresolved issues and those issues go with me until I can resolve them. God has blessed with the uncanny ability to present a positive image through many of life's obstacles.

Another painful situation which demanded me to depend on my faith and spiritual teachings to assist me in managing my behavior was my mother's illness and death. My mother had been caring for her bedridden husband for several years as she personally battled type 1 diabetes and heart disease. Stress is the number 1 killer of diabetics. She was under tremendous stress. I put forth extreme efforts to be there for her and my stepdad. For approximately two years, after work (ending around 5:00 p.m.), I would travel for approximately thirty-five to forty-five minutes from my job in New Jersey to Philadelphia, Pennsylvania, where my parents lived.

I would run errands for meds, groceries, doctor's visits, and trips to the emergency room. Making sincere efforts to lessen the challenges confronting my mother, as she was the main caregiver, often resulted in stress for me. After my daily trips to my parents' home, I would go home around 9:00 or 10:00 p.m., to my husband and teenage daughter. Sadly, my mother, the caregiver, transitioned in July 1998 at the age of seventy-one. Her husband, my stepfather, survived her passing.

I went to work prior to taking my leave of absence, and upon sharing my loss with fellow coworkers, a surprising comment was innocently made. "I didn't know your mother was deathly ill." Later

I thought to myself, how could that be the case, working closely with me side by side, they didn't realize my pain and suffering over such a long period of time (two years).

I was struck with a new reality; my behavior and conversation did *not* provide the external triggers to alert them. How could my behavior be so *misleading?* All was well with me and it wasn't. God and my *spiritual interworkings gave me the strength* to execute much-needed *behaviors* in both situations, domestic and professional.

Thought

The *convictions of one's belief* is demonstrated by how they *interact or react to all others* (self to others). Complimenting your internal *beliefs* through your external expressions of love, appreciation, loyalty and *devotion* is normally related to your spiritual self. Persevere whenever your trials and tribulations seem burdensome and/or overwhelming. From your faith you receive the empowerment to successfully walk through the storm.

No one is useless in!
This world!
Who lightens the
Burden of it
To anyone else.

****

In trying times don't quit trying.
And let us not grow weary in well doing
For in due season, we shall reap,
If we do not lose heart. (Galatians 6:9 RSV)
p.188

13

What Person in Your Life Has Most Influenced/Impacted Your Faith? How?

Influencers reside all around us as we grow and develop into the individuals we present to society. Our cultures, environments, traditions, and families consistently impact growth and development.

From my personal perspective, my faith evolved through the love, guidance, teachings, and beliefs of my mother, Betty L. Webb. She made conscientious efforts to assure that her children were properly exposed to the Word of God and that her children worked diligently to serve. Her nurturing impact was indelible.

My grandmother, Luella Woodland was also an integral part of my nurturing and maturation experience. She too, encouraged the family to engage in the African Methodis Episcopal church doctrines. She worked hard all of her life and always worshipped with us at her side. Her dedication to the church and the Lord were undeniable and we were all the better for it.

As an infant, my mother had me christened Faith Eva Adamson at AME Union Church, on Fairmount Avenue, in Philadelphia, Pennsylvania. That was seventy years ago. I am still a practicing Methodist. The location of the church has moved, but the doctrines remain the same. These doctrines have been embedded in the fabric of my core being.

A multitude of my youth and young adult activities were centered around church, family, and friends. Attending Sunday school and church, along with participating in the choirs, on the usher boards, Young Peoples Department (YPD) consumed most of my weekends. Also I was a server of the palms on Palm Sunday and a member of the Helping Hands. These were venues that provided the growth scenarios to enhance my faith levels. In my adult life, I've served as secretary of the Credit Union, member of the finance committee, missionary, church steward, trustee, Women's Day chairperson, director of Christian Education, and a few more. A great portion of my life has been dedicated to trying to talk the talk and walk the walk.

My mother was extremely instrumental in directing my steps in life and supportive of my endeavors. Subsequently, I recognize her as my number one influence in my life and on my faith.

Thought

Positive influencers will supply the much-needed scope and sequence of behaviors to help a person create their own sense of purpose and fundamental spiritual beliefs. The significance of your inner strength is determined by your foundational faith, which is your virtual prompt to life. My dedication to trying to live the life God, not man, would have me live, has and always will direct my steps.

God plus one!
Is always a majority!
(*God Little Devotional for Women*, 170)

****

If God be for us,
Who can be against us? (Romans 8:31)

14

Does Faith Evoke Miracles?

Miracle is a wonderful and surprising event that is believed to be cause by God…ergo your Higher Power (Google; www.collinsdictionary.com).

I am a firm believer in miracles of faith. Several of my personal experiences mentioned in previous chapters exemplify miracles. I could have met with greater, tragic results in the subway and on the road home from college. It was a miracle I wasn't kidnapped or worse. The car accident could have rendered me maimed or dead. It was the faith, grace, and mercy that prevented the more traumatic outcomes.

Considering the existing obstacles at the time, successfully giving birth to my baby girl was a miracle, like every new life, priceless. She was my miracle baby at 3 lbs. 7oz. (preemie). Faith was a dominant factor in each of these miracles. My faith in what God can do was elevated during these experiences and numerous others not mentioned.

On television, the internet, and in the universe, we are constantly viewing miracles. Earthquake survivors, space travel, technological advancements, scientific inventions, and medical advancements all represent situations of positive unexpected outcomes.

If you are a true believer in the power of your faith, miracles are inevitable.

Thought

Miracles happen each day; the evidence is blatant. There is new life created by the human species, plants, and animals, demonstrating the significance of your faith in the Higher Power. Reproduction yields constant replenishing of the earth. Each miracle has its function and provides the universe with invaluable gifts that maintain the world as an amazing place.

> Jesus replied, "what is impossible with man is possible with God." (Luke 18:27)

> By faith in the name of Jesus, this man whom you see and know was made strong. It is Jesus name and the faith that comes through him that has completely healed, as you can all see. (Acts 3:16)

> God did extraordinary miracles through Paul.
> So that even handkerchiefs and aprons that had touched him were taken to the sick, and their illnesses were cured and the evil spirits left them. (Acts 19:11–12, https://wwwbiblestudy tools.com)

15

Are You Currently Struggling with a Self-to-Self Conflict? Explain

My life, as of January 28, 2018, changed forever. My husband, whom I met in 1969 when I was twenty-one, married him 1970 at the tender age of twenty-two, lived and grew old with him for forty-seven years, at which time he transitioned to life eternal.

As a completely grown adult, I am in uncharted waters. I have to make some major life decisions to successfully transition into my new normal, without my constant friend, protector, and love.

Tony Robbins stated, "The quality of life, is the quality of your relationships." I agree as I reflect on our time together, and it was a really good life. He would only want the best for me as I move forward. My faith encourages and empowers me to face my realities and act accordingly.

Taking a leap of faith, I will make decisions about where I choose to live, here or elsewhere. Health maintenance issues, personal possessions to be distributed (when and to whom), and home renovations are issues of importance that I need to resolve. My faith will guide me through it all.

Renewing my memberships, affiliations, and connections to some of my former organizations will motivate me, to strive to be a more productive woman of purpose and service to others. On the lighter side, travel has always been exciting to me. My husband and

I made travel an integral part of our relationship, and I intend to continue to engage.

Tim Storey, an ordained minister, author (nine books), and life coach, once said, "When in the midst of your setback (biggest challenge), God is already preparing your comeback." So as usual, I'm putting my future in the hands of God. As an optimist, I know God never shuts one door without opening another that is more glorious and fulfilling than the last.

Thought

People awaken each day, not knowing what the day entails; various events are put in their paths. Some are delightful, joyous, and victorious; other experiences not so positive. Death, poverty, illness, and devastation are just a few of the negative occurrences. We take a leap of faith each time we make a move (professional, economic, domestic, emotional), make a decision, or make plan of action. Our faith determines the outcomes.

God always gives
His best
To those who leave!
The choice with Him!
(*God Little Devotional Book for Women*, 272)

****

Blessed be the Lord,
Who daily loadeth us with benefits,
even the God of our salvation! (Psalm 68:19)

16

Can You Identify a Self-to-Others Issue? How Will You Address the Situation?

Faith has undeniably impacted my interactions and reactions to people in my space. Currently, I am making a sincere and conscientious effort to acknowledge all others as individuals on a mission to honor their faith via their living and their giving.

Subsequently, serving others and focusing on their well-being through my actions is my goal. Making determinations concerning how to basically "pay it forward" is my self-to-others dilemma. A multitude of options are available. How I can best serve the masses with my particular skill set, must be established?

Writing this book was one method; encouraging the use of faith groups (discussions on faith) to help us talk the talk and walk the walk of faith is another. I will use these tools to enhance the well-being of others. The recognition and complete acceptance of their faith practices is foundational to improved self-to-self and self-to-others relationships.

Brainstorming possible other alternatives is my present status. Working with faith-based organizations is definitely a consideration among others. I feel compelled to take a leap of faith and choose faith over fear. The verse from the book of Luke 12:48 is embedded in the fabric of my soul:

> But he that knew not, and did commit
> things worthy of stripes, shall be beaten with full

stripes. For unto whomsoever much given, of him shall be much required: and to whom men have committed much, they will ask the more. (KJV)

Thought:

Love is the most powerful spirit in life, and faith is its greatest promoter. Your love, kindness, trust, and mercy shown to all others makes for a greater display of humanity throughout the world.

You may give
Without loving
But you cannot love
Without giving.

****

For God so loved the world, that he gave
His only begotten Son, that whosoever
believeth in him should not perish,
But have everlasting life.
John 3:16. (p. 18)

****

We should seize
Every opportunity to give encouragement.
Encouragement is the oxygen to the soul.
A man hath joy by the answer of his mouth.
And a word spoken in due season, how good it is
Proverb 15:23
God's Little Devotional Book for Women (p. 16)

****

God never asks
about our ability
Or our inability
just our
Availability

****

I heard the voices. Of the Lord, saying,
Whom shall I send, and who will go for us?
Then said I, Here am I; send me.
(Isaiah: 6:8)

17

Reflections

Describe what you have internalized on this faith journey.
How will this experience effect how you
approach life and the people in it?

Impetuous action and reactions may frequently occur if we don't indulge in critical thinking as it relates to how we treat ourselves and one another. The Gospel, as taught by the prophets, the twelve disciples, and Jesus, the Son of God direct ultimately should direct *the* paths of the believers. Humans err; it is a proven fact.

But fortunately, our Father is a God of second chances, and it is imperative that mankind doesn't drown in complacency. Human beings can relish in the idea that God (or your Higher Power) is a forgiving God, but he is also a vengeful God. Efforts to live by his Word are key to pleasing the Almighty and exhibiting behaviors that praise and sanctify his holiness.

Trust, confidence, strong inspirational beliefs/doctrines, and certitude are the ingredients of a powerful faith that provides assurances and strength. Compliances to the spiritual teachings and affirmations of faith compel man to live a life of faithfulness.

Projecting a possible life of altruism, or the like thereof, as I venture into my new reality may be far more challenging than I might think. I am earnestly struggling with the how. Transformations are inevitable, if the transition and the personal services are to be successfully instituted and implemented.

Impatience can foil the plan. Structure, trust, and confidence must be employed if the vision is to be manifested in a timely manner. I know my faith will be a phenomenal facet of my endeavor.

My self-to-self (self-introspection) and self-to-others (treatment toward others) will be hugely connected as I advance into my life of service. Paying it forward has its just rewards. We must always remember during our faith journey the following:

> Let each one do just as he has
> resolved in his heart,
> Not grudgingly or under compulsion, for God
> loves a cheerful giver. (2 Corinthians 7:9)

18

Create Your Own Affirmation(s) on Faith

Your faith is your invisible and spiritual power source.
It allows you to eliminate obstacles and alter situations.

Cherish and manage your visions and let your
faith in God be your wings. Soar!

Faith in God and yourself increases your
worthiness and sense of purpose.

Shout it out for the world to hear,
"Oh, my faith, my faith in God delivers me."

Live and share your faith and truth. All will improve.

Devastate hate and perpetuate your faith.

Live your godly faith without hesitation.

DR. FAITH E. HARTIE

Faith in God rules!

May our faith in God be sufficient to
eliminate the practice of number 45.
Children be ripe from the arms of their
mothers is not the American way!

Obliterate *hate*! Perpetuate *love* and *faith*!

Daily Inspirational Thoughts

Feeling Thoughtful

Good, spontaneous, yet specific **Sunday:**

God grants us moments of spontaneity, but the specific choices made during those experiences have both good and bad consequences.

Take a second and make a wise choice!
The choice may change your life forever!
Use your faith in God!

Feeling Inspired

Good, sensitivity, and spectacular **Saturday:**

Our faith grants us sensitivity to the needs of others. We love, care, educate, and shelter them as needed.

Spectacular and wholesome relationships develop and evolve over time because of the meaningful, heartwarming, and sensitive experiences we share.

Sensitivity Rules!

Feeling Hopeful

Good-favored and faith-filled **Friday:**

Awakening to a new day of favor and faithfulness is a God-given gift. Go forth and share the goodness.

Care and Share!

Feeling Refreshed

Good, tasteful, and thought-filled **Thursday:**

Our lives require strong faith, structure, calm, love, and peace. These pillars help us manage emotions when life gets chaotic, frustrating, and depressing.

Faith Protects and Provides

Feeling Energized

Good worthy **Wednesday:**

Propel your worthy faith practices into the atmosphere, so they serve to:

> *encourage*
> *engage*
> *empower*

All to be...the best they can!

Feeling Motivated

Good trouble-free **Tuesday:**

If you have a thorn in your side today, be it medical, mental, emotional, or financial, look to God. Our faith in our heavenly Father will remove it!

God's Got *You*!

Feeling Concerned

Good masterful **Monday:**

Embrace our Master and faith to overcome challenges. We all stand in the need of prayer!

Feeling Blessed

Good, sacred, and sweet **Sunday:**

Live your faith, truth, and sacred purpose with a sweet and giving heart.
Perpetuate goodness!

Feeling Grateful

Good, stable, and sincere **Saturday:**

Our God and faith guide us to lives that are stable and sincere.

Feeling Inspired

Good, festive, and fab **Friday:**

Faith, festivities, and fabulosity make a great weekend! Live that life!

Feeling Loved

Good trust-filled **Thursday:**

Spread trust and love through faithful deeds!
Trust God.
He's the answer!

Feeling Positive

Good wisdom **Wednesday:**

God provides us experiences in life resulting in the development of wisdom.
Let's use it wisely!

Feeling Strong

Good, merciful, and methodical **Monday:**

Our lives are filled and always blessed with God's mercy. Our lives are enhanced by proven methods that provide: order, purpose, focus, progress, beauty, and stability.

What Is Today's Method?

Feeling Motivated

Good, spiritual, and serious **Sunday:**

Shout out our serious issues.
Use your faith in God and mankind to make positive *change*!

Feeling Determined

Good, sweet, and sincere **Saturday:**

Speak your truth to power.
Living your sincerest truth powerfully!
Actions equals power!

Feeling Energized

Good, feasible, and favored **Friday:**

Cast your fears and problems to the heavens.
Embrace your fearless faith and God's favor!
God Rules!

Feeling Thankful

Good thrifty **Thursday:**

Encourage and empower thrift to strengthen your economy!

Feeling Inspired

Good work-filled **Wednesday:**

Strong faith and hard.

Other Quotes

You have to go to the corner
On faith
And faith will see you
Around the corner.
(Grandmother of Shirley Clay)

Personal Experiences

Indeed, my husband and I were married for twenty-three
years, divorced for seven years, and then remarried in
2000. I teased him that I gave *him* a second chance.
(Merrill-Jean Bailey)

****

Because I am often pragmatic, I like to see what is around
the corner. But when I don't know what is around the corner,
I solidly rely on my faith in God. I believe that everything
works together for the good, for those that love the Lord.
That has carried me through 72 years of living, and
I know it will carry me the rest of the way.
(Merrill-Jean Bailey)

****

Dr. Faith on Faith

Motto:
My faith
Your faith
Our faith
Changes Things

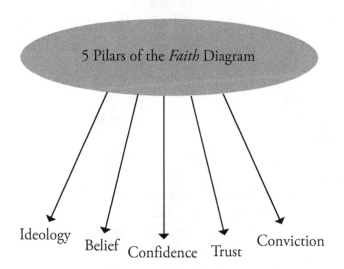

5 Pilars of the *Faith* Diagram

Ideology Belief Confidence Trust Conviction

Faith and the Light of God's Rainbow

Rainbow: water droplets that break through the white sunlight into seven colors of the spectrum:

Red
Orange
Yellow
Green
Blue
Indigo
Violet

Jazmine's story: leukemia
Jazmine, a sixteen-year-old at the time was diagnosed with leukemia.

Living the life of a child of God in the light of the rainbow is a journey of his children. The Bible mentions the rainbow several times. It is believed that the "rainbow is the sign from the Almighty that we are not forgotten."

In Genesis it is described as a sign of God's mercy as well as the pact/covenant God made with Noah that such a flood would not be sent again.

In Ezekiel 1:26–28, colors of the rainbow are compared to the glory of God while in Revelation, Apostle John compares the rainbow colors to the glory or power of God.

Noah teaches mankind the seven basic rules to adhere to con-
forming to the seven colors of the rainbow:

Noahide Laws: Seven colors of the rainbow remind us of them!

Dr. Faith on Faith by Dr. Faith E. Hartie

- Thou shall not worship idols.
- Thou shall not commit blaspheme.
- Thou shall not murder.
- Thou shall not have immoral relationships.
- Thou shall not steal.
- Thou shall respect all living creatures.
- Thou shall set up courts of law.

(Colors of the Rainbow and their Meanings: The Bible and the
colors of the Rainbow https://www.colormeanings.com)

Significance of colors of the rainbow in modern philosophy:

Red: first color; signifies passion, vitality, enthusiasm, and security.
Orange: second color: signifies creativity, practicality, playfulness, as
    well as equilibrium and control.
Yellow: third color; signifies clarity of thought, wisdom, orderliness,
    and energy.
Green: fourth and middle color of the rainbow; signifies fertility,
    growth, balance, health, and wealth.
Blue: fifth color; signifies the color of the sky and the wide oceans
    and is associated with spirituality and divinity.
Indigo: sixth color; signifies that where blue is calming, indigo is
    sedating. Indigo is mystical as it bridges the gap between finite
    and infinite. Indigo-colored gemstones are often used for spiri-
    tual attainment, psychic abilities, self-awareness, and enhance-
    ment of intuition.
Violet: seventh color; it is considered the highest level of spirituality.
    It can ignite one's imagination and be an inspiration to an artist.

Dark tones of violet are associated with sorrow. Deeper tones of violet or purple denote high spiritual mastery.

I was once told a story about a rainbow sighting on the ceiling, in the room of a sick person. My relative was in the room with the patient and also experienced the miraculous sighting. Within months the cancer was in recession. God's power at work in a mystical aura. Years later, the patient is still in good health.

Thought

Philosophically the actuality and significance of the rainbow is comprehensible as it relates to faith and mankind. The colors red, orange, yellow, blue, indigo, and violet connect to the key elements of faith.

Passion (red), control (orange), wisdom and energy (yellow), fertility and health (green), spirituality and divinity (blue), self-awareness and enhancement of intuition (indigo), and high spiritual mastery are some of the fundamental characteristics of mankind.

We continuously strive to identify and fulfill our passion(s) in life. Control is a significant element to the foundation of life. We seek and internalize wisdom for better lives, and the energy force is responsible for our pursuit of a good life. Fertility allows for the continued replenishing of the universe, and our health is vital to our psychological, physical, and emotional stability.

Our spirituality is the body of the faith we own and through which we thrive. Self-awareness keeps us connected the aspirations, expectations, and foundational purpose of self. Finally the high spiritual mastery sustains our faith in God, life, and beyond.

The rainbow colors reflect and resonate lights of life and faith and represents the glory of God's power and those that cherish his Word.

"God will never forget them."

Faith and Hope

Faith generates and regenerates hope
Faith and hope inspire all mankind
Faith is our spiritual scope
We depend on our faith during life's journey
Hope and faith we lean on, all the time

Men, women, children too
All look to God for words of faith, 'tis true
Hope rekindles sparks in life
Faith rekindles hope
Hope rekindles faith

Hope and faith
We as a people must embrace
Both will stimulate,
They will motivate,
Both will cultivate the human race

God's gifts to us all, faith and hope
Our realities

Part 2

Your Faith

Contributors

1. Dr. Carol Cantu Educator/Administrator, Author, Entrepreneur
2. Ms. Maryilyn Jamal Educator/Administrator, Regional Director of So. Jersey Teen Shop
3. Ms. Annece Hart, Educator
4. Ms. Sherrae' L. Hartie. Psych. Therapist, Educator, Entrepreneur
5. Pastor, Rev. Shane Hartie, Realtor, Educator
6. Ms. Dawn Webb, Social Worker

Your Faith

1. What is faith to you?

As you journey through life, connecting to people is a major part of the journey experience. Family, friends, and others make up dynamics of human relationships. Several of the people in my life's circle have graciously shared some of their most intimate "faith moments."

> Faith to me is believing in what you cannot see before it becomes manifested or visible to the eye. Believing what is right in front of you is actually you just believing in what already exist. However if you put your trust in God, believe on His promises, stand on His words, and believe on what you can't see, but know that it will happen in God's timing…that to me is faith.
>
> —Annece Adamson Hart
> Educator

> Faith to me is the absolute assurance, the absolute knowledge, and the unshakable confidence that God is in control of my life in every way, with everyone, and at all times. Often this control is not in the direction that I want. It is not always what I prayed for and is often surprising. But knowing that he is in control, usually brings me a sense of peace and joy. I say usually because when his will is not in the direction of

my will, I have experienced confusion and sometimes sadness.

For a while, at one time, I mistook the sadness for lack of faith, but now I realize my faith was not shaken, but my joy was interrupted. It sometimes takes a while for me to realize, just as little children, that even though I may not understand his decisions, he knows what is best. I may not understand for a long time, I may not understand until as the Gospel song reminds me, I'll understand better and by and by. But just knowing that whatever happen, it is under God's control. It keeps me sane, mentally healthy, and willing to keep on keeping on.

—Dr. Carol Cantu
Educator, author, speaker, entrepreneur

Faith is the ability to believe in what is not physically or scientifically justified or proven and also it is a degree of trust that you have in a certain outcome, person place or thing being or behaving in a certain way based on how they have done so in the past. My faith encompasses me computing a bunch of facts, experiences, possibilities, and hopes into my thinking process that gives me what I am almost sure will happen, believe will happen, and hope will happen. I have faith in me, my family, my friends, mankind, nature, science, and a higher power that works for the greater good of all. Faith is definitely something I feel in many areas of my life and struggle to increase and some others. My experiences affect my vacillating beliefs and therefore I am always hoping for events and people on my journey to positively make me a more faith-filled person.

—Sherrae L. Hartie, Psy. MS
Empowerment coach, mental health
counselor, motivational speaker

Faith is believing in an outcome or someone. It is having the confidence that someone or a situation will bring about a favorable or the best result. Faith is an attitude one maintains even when situations or people don't appear to align to yield favorable or the best results. Faith is trust.

—Dawn Webb
Social worker

Faith is the substance of things hopes for and the evidence of things not seen (Hebrews 11:1). Faith to me begins with hearing truth. This truth births hope within us and we then start living in a way that promotes a manifestation of the desired outcome.

—Shane Hartie
Pastor, educator, realtor

Total confidence, belief and trust in God for the unseen…my faith causes me to believe in the impossible.

—Marilyn S. Jamal
Educator, Teen Shop Sooth
Jersey regional director

2. What are your four strong areas of faith? (Provide two personal experiences.)

I am not sure how to label the areas of my faith, but I know that my faith seems to be stronger when I realize that I am not out of ideas, options, or creative ways to solve problems. Then this is when I say that this is Red Sea situation.

When the Egyptians were behind the Israelites in the wilderness, another were mountain on both sides of them, and there was only the Red Sea before them; they're out of options. There was nothing they could do. That's when faith has to be strong. We have to know that God's got it. It has happened to me many times. The experiences are tied in my book *On My Way*.

Mia, my daughter was a junior at the academy. She was faced with the most challenging course she would have in high school chemistry. Her chemistry teacher had a reputation for being demanding.

During bible study, Mia had learned to claim Bible promises and had chosen as one of her favorite Bible test Proverbs 16:30. The night before school was to begin, the family opened the Bible to this test, read it and personalized it. We claimed it as a promise, and fervently prayed that God would guide Mia to do all in her power to be successful in chemistry. And when her limited powers ran out that He would supply whatever was needed to bring success.

The text clearly says that God would help her plan succeed. Her part was to have a plan. So Mia, secured a student tutor. She designated a regular study time and place, and she studied each evening, San though there were going to be a test the next day; she did not wait until tests were announced to begin studying.

It was indeed challenging. But Mia succeeded in the class. On a few occasions the she actually scored an "A" on the test, we had family celebrations. God kept his promise because in prayer we committed our plans to Him. The promise is still there and can be renewed upon request. (Dr. Carol Cantu, *Prayer Changes Things*, 1–2)

My four strongest areas of faith are in my family to love me no matter what, my friends too support me and most of my endeavors, my education to supply me with knowledge, options and opportunities, and my Higher Power to protect and guide me. My faith may not always be so strong in the latter as I have seen that "God's plan" isn't always aligned with my own, especially detail for detail. I simply hope and pray that whoever is making the big decisions, the Great "I am" wants what I want. I certainly feel with a great level of faith that no matter what has happened, my best interest and that of those around me, whom I love, is kept in mind and that that power or being is routing for me and my success.
—Sherrae' L. Hartie

A. God: my father in heaven loves, created, and sustains me and all that I am. I have a faith that I will see him one day because of the sacrifice that his Son made on the cross for my sins.

B. Family: I know that my family loves me. I have depended on them for guidance support comfort and corrections.

C. Life: life is hard and at times not fair but I notice that when I mess up, life still keeps moving on allowing me to take another try.

D. Self: I learned that if I keep pushing and loving that good can come forward even out of messy situations.

I have been through a rough divorce. I have found that God still loves me and that he gave me the strength and permission to keep moving forward. Even when I thought at times that marrying again could have bad results too, I just had faith that my Lord can do better. I'm remarried with an amazing wife and beautiful children. Raising children can be tough, but I have faith for their future.

In 1999, I wanted to be ordained. I kept working to do so, but it never happened. I would not want to give up on this dream. Years and life passed and I felt didn't think much about is. Finally and after the Lord put me in the right place, the opportunity came back around. I was ordained and I'm very active in my church. Amen!

—Shane Hartie

"Be strong and of good courage, do not fear nor be afraid of them; for the Lord your God, He is the One who goes with you. He will not leave you nor forsake you" (Deuteronomy 31:6).

I've learned to trust in God's promises for his children. Life altering challenges can often cause us to question God, worry and doubt our faith. "Why me, Lord?" or "Why not me, Lord?" Two questions that I no longer struggle with as I trust God to see me through.

Hoping for a promotion, I struggled when others around me were being promoted and I was not. Every day, I expressed my disappointment with my dear friend and colleague, asking why not me. I walked into her office one day after numerous conversations and complaints and stated that I had let it go and had given it to God. The conversation this day was based on my acknowledgment that impatience, and not totally waiting and trusting in God, was the issue.

For everyone who asks receives; he who seeks finds; and to him who knocks, the door will be opened (Matthew 7:8).

Reflecting on his word, letting go and letting God, my faith, I received the promotion within the next few weeks. When I received the call, it was so far from my thoughts that I asked if I could report at another time due to a previous appointment.

Delight yourself also in the LORD; and he shall give you the desires of your heart (Psalm 37:4).

—Marilyn S. Jamal

3. What is one area of your faith to be strengthened?

Because I have experienced my joy being stolen, I know Satan is behind it. I want to have such strong faith that when my will is not God's will and I experience disappointment, I don't lose my joy. This does not mean that I don't expect to have grief or pain or even sadness (I know this is earth and who is the prince of earth), but I want these temporary experiences to be fast fleeting and for the rainbow at the end of the storm to always been view or at least expected.

—Dr. Carol Cantu

If any area of my faith could be strengthened, I would pray for it to be my faith in my protection, that I would go unharmed. I am scared of putting myself in harm's way, and that keeps me from doing many things. I certainly travel less and go fewer places out of fear that I might step into a situation where something might happened that would alter the course of

my life in a negative way. I wish I had faith that
many decisions weren't life and death situations
but that everything would have a safe result.

—Sherrae' H.

Does your faith give you an extraordinary sense of power and
peace?

Yes, my faith in God gives me an extraordinary sense of power and peace because my faith
has allowed me to transition from believing and
having confidence to actually experiencing the
manifestation of my faith or belief. Since my
faith has produced the favorable or best results
for me in life, I now know surrendering and having faith in God gives me strength to face and
overcome life's daily challenges. The power is in
surrendering to God and with the surrendering
comes the peace. Peace is the result of knowing
God will work all things out again just like *he* did
before and the result will be best for me.

—Dawn W.

I believe that I need to strengthen the ability
to try new things. I want to become comfortable
with some of the unknown things.

—Shane H.

I need to listen more to God and speak less
(Hebrews 11:3). By faith we understand that the
universe was created by the word of God so that
what is seen was not made out of things that are
visible. Raised by my aunt and living in a home
with my grandmother, one generation removed
from slavery, her words of wisdom ring loudly
and ever present in my ear. She would tell me

often, especially when I was being anxious or unquiet, "Baby, be still and listen to God." I reflect on those words today when my spirit is unquiet, I sit still, read his word, and listen to God.

—Marilyn S. Jamal

4. Do you think American society is faith based? If yes, explain. Give three examples.

I am not sure about America. When I compare it to other countries I have visited or lived in, I say yes. Compared to Europe, America seems to be faith based. But compared to some third-world countries, America is not. People that have a lot think they are in control and that their privilege and wealth are the results of what they have done. They think that the schools they have attended, the jobs they have worked, the business sense they have developed are all the results of their own efforts, talents, and intelligence. They tend to give themselves the credit, and they depend on themselves for greater advancements. There is little acknowledgment of God or their faith in God. I notice that poor people have to depend on God. They see how he works in their lives, and they give him the glory and he increases their faith. I have seen more poor people in the third world, thus I have seen more faith in the third world.

When friends from all over the world have visited me, one of things they have noticed is the abundance of houses of worship. The Europeans see it as a sign that we are a faith-based country. Africans, Asians, and Middle Easterners see it as a contradiction. They say, how can a country with such high crime and immoral behavior have so many places of worship?

—Dr. Carol Cantu

I believe that America is definitely a faith-based society that includes faith as it pertains to religion. First of all, America is a country whose colonies were founded by people in pursuit of religious freedom, the freedom to believe and have faith in whatever they wanted. In their case it was "The God of Abraham." They were puritans. They left England, especially the church of England and all its usurpations, to create this place where we, Americans, can live "freely" and are "free" to believe in and generally practice any religion we choose.

Our current beliefs have all stemmed from there to the various religions we practice today. The more people who come to America, the more religions pop up. I think we may not believe in the same things, but most Americans feel more comfortable with the notion that the people around them have faith in something greater than themselves. Also, America still has money that reads "in God we trust," so most people interact with America's faith all day long with every exchange of currency.

Secondly, Americans have faith in their government. We trust that we will always be protected by those in power for the most part and that we can change who is in power if we feel they aren't serving the citizens well. For in this time of Trumpism, there would be even more anarchy and chaos than we are currently seeing if Americans believed us all to be stuck with no recourse and no changes would ever come. American citizens trust the process of checks and balances to work for the greater good of the people, eventually, which is why on November 6, 2018, many people will be going out to vote for their decided best candidate to place in various positions of government. We believe change is possible!

We, the American people have faith to hopefully empower our newly elected officials to go forth and make changes to remedy our country's ails and current circumstances, lifestyles and standards for which many believe to be eroding due to ineffective governing practices and corruption. We believe we can make it better if we follow the laws and work within the system. I hope we are right.

Americans also have faith in a culture, a way of being, a set of rules and standards that most of us should abide by and uphold as "good" Americans. Acting outside of these traits is considered "unAmerican." We are to do no harm to others, protect what is ours within the boundaries of the law, work hard or intelligently to positively contribute to and take care of American society, our communities, our homes, ourselves, and our kin. We are expected to respect other people's persons, places, and things. We are the "good guys" who help out when we can, even if it strains us a little. We believe in being the hero of our own stories. We trust other Americans to operate within these expected norms. It is the American way. At least it is spiritually, but financially, it becomes much less black and white.

Americans believe in capitalism. It's an arena of finance where money is its own god and people have faith in what it can do for them. It can lift you up quickly if you are good at it and positioned well to begin with, but its outcomes vary. In capitalism people are allowed to be much more ruthless. It sustains a more "survival of the fittest" mentality where a person is allowed to do most anything legal to win the "game." It has a different set of ethics and morals. People can buy and sell each other's companies and workers in very hostile manners; they will figuratively slaughter an opponent in business. Capitalism is a game anyone can play but it tends to be drastically life altering and less fun for the losers. This is where two sides of our culture enter into a gray area because what happens in business often trickles out of the arena of sport for profit and affect workers and families who can't afford to be playing the games with their money at all. These Americans are people who go to work to eat and survive not to play and win at a game they can't afford to lose. American people have faith that the government will even the playing field enough to protect the average workers, those whom, whether the wish it to be or not, are pawns in the games of the powerful wealthy elite.

—Sherrae' H.

I don't think America is very faith based. We have so much that not much is left for creativity and desire. We are inundated with a digital lifestyle that allows us to see anything we desire.

—Shane H.

Yes, I do! Faith-based organizations are relentless in the belief that they have a religious obligation to help the poor and disadvantaged. I found the history of their origin for several of them fascinating, as is their longevity and sus-

tainability. I am also perplexed that in research-
ing the effectiveness of these programs, because
of my own curiosity, statistical data has not been
updated in some areas since 2014. My curiosity
has peaked and I plan to continue with additional research in this area.

—Marilyn S. Jamal

Through their mission statements, vision statements, and current outreach, included in my response, and the thousands of volunteers that support these programs, I believe that they exhibit their
faith through their works.

Salvation Army is currently one of the largest social services pro-
viders in the world, running homeless shelters, community centers,
disaster relief programs, and thrift stores in 118 countries.

USAID leads international development and humanitarian
efforts to save lives, reduce poverty, strengthen democratic gover-
nance, and help people progress beyond assistance.

The American Red Cross prevents and alleviates human suffering in the face of emergencies by mobilizing the power of volunteers
and the generosity of donors.

5. How can faith impact personal situations? Share a personal situation for each.

Job

After I had retired and ten months of bliss,
I was asked to come out of retirement to help
start new Christian school in Philadelphia. Deep
down I really wanted to continue sleeping late
following the beat of my own drummer, collect-
ing retirement checks and social security. How
could I beat that? I believed that the people calling me really needed me. I prayed and fasted and
asked God to speak to me loudly and clearly. He

did. I knew it was him impressing me to go to Philadelphia and help launch the new school. My faith said it was God and he was emphatic about it.

After the beginning to work in Philadelphia, I learned that the people on the job really need me, not because of my preconceived idea they had about my outstanding skill or experiences, but because of my patience. The job was not hard, but tedious. It took a lot of faith and a lot of patience.

But more than that, my brother and his family in Philadelphia needed me. Allen was so sick, his daughter Sherrae' had moved home to help her mom with her dad's care, but she ruptured her Achilles heel. I was there, and it became clear to me that being there to help with Allen's care was what God wanted more than need for the school. I was able to help the school, I increased my loving relationship with my brother, my sister-in-law, and my niece, and other Philadelphia relatives. I was blessed so profoundly by these experiences, and my faith was increased, as well as my joy.

—Dr. Carol Cantu

Faith can impact a life by magnitudes if only you believe. In my opinion my life would be in shambles if I did not have faith in God. I believe that every word that God speaks is true. Even when you go through difficult or tragic times in life, having faith in the Word of God can make you realize that even in the midst of all that you are going through, you can still make it. I can remember a time when I was one of many people when I received a layoff slip from a former employer out of the blue...no rhyme nor reason. I did not have a plethora of latenesses and absences, nor did I have written reprimands. I had previously been Teacher of the Year, Teacher of the Month, and was very involved in curriculum activities. One morning, I overheard I was being relieved of my duties. What? Me? What's going on here? All I could come up with is that's time of year when they needed to play Eeny, Meeny, Miny, Moe while shifting people's livelihoods upside down with no plan of how it was going to affect all who were involved, including themselves.

Now, I could have definitely lost faith because at that point, I was losing my job and I am a child of God. I was not understanding why this is happening. That would mean in our household would be the only one generating a steady income until I found, which turned out to be more difficult than one could ever imagine. Our son was involved in a lot of extracurricular activities that I was paying for and he also had to go to many medical appointments that needed copays. I am human, so I was nervous at times. I was aggravated and furious at what was happening. Without getting into all the details, just know that I felt stress because I did not know where this was coming from nor what I end up doing. Nevertheless, I chose not to let go of my faith. The Bible says that "what the devil means for evil, God will turn it around for my good." It never says that we won't go through stuff in life. We are human. Things will come our way, but it is how we respond to them that guarantees the results that we want.

If I decided to speak negatively about my situation, listen to the naysayers, moped around, or threw in the towel, my experience would have been either more difficult or fruitless. Instead I prayed and fasted. I reminded God of what he promised me in his word if I had faith and trusted in him.

I researched, I interviewed, and I was actually getting ready to take a job did not want. Right before that happened, I received a call from my previous employer, asking me to return for the upcoming year. I had to have faith that God would supply my every need. I am thankful and he did!

—Annece Hart

Relationship

When I think about faith in relationships, my mind ventures back to college. I had been in some relationships that were of no good quality, so I decided to take a break and focus on getting myself together. I wanted to be a better me. I was into the Word of God more, living life without many responsibilities as of yet, was traveling to various destinations with friends, and figuring out my new teaching career. I was feeling great. One night my cousins, some friends, and I decided to go to a youth event at a familiar church. I was there having a good time, not realizing that someone had their eye on me.

I received a phone call a few days later due to this admirer's inquiries about me, and asking if he could get my number. Honestly, it truly threw me off because this person and I had known each other since we were little. I never has an interest but was suddenly "slightly intrigued." "Sure, why not. Let's see if we could have some fun," I said. Big mistake. It started out a little oddly but nothing that seemed to be alarming. To make a long "short" story even shorter, this relationship that only lasted four months felt like an eternity because of the emotional rollercoaster of a ride.

After I got into the relationship, there were so many red flags that I couldn't imagine were possibly all true. I was minding my business and extremely happy being in the place that I was before he popped into my world. What was happening here? I will refrain from giving many details out of respect to the other person who was involved; just know that I was devastated that I had allowed someone with so muchness into my life!

Now in this situation, I was slightly depressed, hurt, and confused when things began to come to light because it felt like a whirlwind of events. My faith took a hit and had questions. However, I am not the one to wait until questions are answered to make a choice, if it is detrimental to my peace of mind because I trusted God to make everything come to right for me regardless of what I was going through and I heeded his warnings. God truly blessed me to escape a rocky road that would have led to devastation. I severed that relationship faster than the young man could blink. Even though I was hurting, I knew I had done the right thing. I felt a weight lift off as soon as I cut of communications. When I mean all, I mean *all* communications. Nothing but having faith in God can help you to have the strength to stand up and be strong when you feel weak and confused. I was able to walk away and had my head up high. God will not make you be ashamed when you have faith in him.

—Annece Hart

Faith is developed through a means of interacting with others. Based on how they have behaved in the past, I can guess what they will most likely do in the present or future. This knowledge forwards me a sense of trust and that trust allows me to determine a person's role in my life. I have faith in a person to be themself; I have an expectation for a consistency of their abilities, thoughts, and behaviors. When they step outside of their expected norms, resulting in negative outcomes, I lose faith in them and my hopes for the role they can positively play in my life are diminished.

Once upon a time, I was at an event and a "friend" left me stranded, waiting for a ride on a corner in a populated downtown area. I wasn't in danger, and I found a way home, but what I learned that day is that that that person would abandon me if they decided it was, not simply to their detriment because that I might expect but to their convenience or entertainment. Once you know this about a person, their role must be changed. It was downgraded that day, never to fully recover. It wasn't about forgiveness; it was about trust. I still have faith in them to be who they have always been, that that is a part of their character and it would take something I don't have to change it. I knew they would do it again if convenient to them and that is a person you know, a person you can enjoy, but not a person on whom you can rely. I currently think of this person as family but are we friends, not so much.

—Sherrae' H.

Spiritual

This one can be very tricky and at times complicated for many people, even Christians. Many people have faith to an extent but don't know how to fully exercise it. They do to understand how to make their faith work for the by truly living and using God's principles the way that he intended for us to operate in them. Many believe that we have to beg and plead with God for things to happen in our lives. We do have to do that. Religion can tend to make it more difficult than it really is.

Yes, he definitely wants us to let our request be made or down to him, and he definitely wants us to have faith, but here is the kicker: what we are requesting, he already made happen for us. Surprise? That how much he loves us. One scripture in the Bible that pops into my mind: "Let us therefore come boldly to the throne of grace, that we may obtain mercy and find grace to help us in time of need." Every part of this scripture is true.

However, what we fail to realize even in this that when Jesus died on the cross over 2000 years ago, not only did he take all of the blame for the negative things of the world, like sin, disease, and eternal death. But in exchange he gave us eternal life, the keys to his kingdom, and the power to all believers. He did everything he was going to do for us on that day.

All blessings, all favor, all the healing, all the rescuing, all the promotions, all the making a way out of no way, all of it was done back then. He prefers for us as his kids to use the power that he has bestowed upon us, along with us having faith, to call for the things that we need forth. He has given us the ability to do so because of our belief in him. The scripture above says, "let us come forward boldly to the throne of grace that we may obtain mercy and find grace." It did not say obtain the things that we need from him to do simply because it's already been done by the finished works of the cross. We must stand on our faith, remind God of his promises through his Word by speaking it back to him, call these words forth and believe that he will do it.

—Annece Hart

I have faith in a greater power than myself and I refer to that power as God. I believe it is everywhere and in everything, that it is a life force, an energy which simply is. It exist in forms we humans experience with our five senses, our sixth sense, and in ways beyond our perception. I do not have the most steady faith in any particular religion's capability to be the alpha and omega of all there is to know about God, man, nor beast, but I feel that God is fluid and infinite beyond our understanding. I am a Christian by birth, and I practice and appreciate both Christianity and Buddhist philosophy, rarely finding conflicts between the two and feeling generally spiritually fulfilled. I hope I am heard when I pray and I am hearing responses, wisdom, and Gospel when I meditate.

I practice being of God and with God simultaneously and attempt to protect that practice, existence, or experience from the corruptions of "men" who may sometimes profess to know God yet insert their will into religion with hopes of personal profit. I search for and live in a connection and truthful communing with the God that is outside of myself and from within that no man can put asunder. I have faith in my being, having been made from that great source, "the creator" or the "beer." I have faith that as an extension of that greatness that I am also great and here in human form to continue being great, manifesting greatness, and to do great things. I believe in my ability to connect with God spiritually using my sixth sense through distancing myself from anything overwhelming my other five senses. I meditate, but I also recognize God in everything beautiful I see or experience too. Although my interactions may feel differently from one day to the next, it is always good.

I have come to a point in my life where I have no expectations of God—only hopes, prayers, and open ears.

—Sherrae' H.

A. Job. As a realtor, my every paycheck depends on how I produce. I pray and listen for direction. I see myself increasing in unorthodox ways to real estate when I stay close to my Father in heaven.

B. Relationship. I have seen that the more that I serve, the more people around me follow. I am the head of my home and other areas, so I am the first to serve. I saw that in Jesus and in my earthly father. It really does work better that way.

C. Spiritual. The more that I engage my Father in heaven and to be obedient to his Word and way, I get to see the most amazing things manifest in my personal life.

—Shane H.

Before becoming more intense in thoughts on faith (because of Dr. Faith) I would have said that I have strong faith. I would probably have said in God alone do I have absolute faith. But I have faith, absolute faith in my family. I know that my family has my back. They would not do anything intentionally to bring me harm. If I need something that they could give, I know they would give it. I know their love for me is genuine and used on our relationship through the years. Does this mean that every single person who has a blood linked to me I don't want to name names here, but the ones who are included here, know who they are.

They are the same ones that have faith in me. Some friends are in the same category as family. They too know who they are.

—Dr. Carol Cantu

I have faith that Jesus is Lord. He loves me and has died for my sins. I have faith that one day I will see my place in his kingdom. Have faith in my family. Even if things get tough, we will be there for each other. I have faith that I am not perfect and that I don't need to be perfect and that helps me to relax.

—Shane H.

6.   Do you have faith? In what? In who?

Yes, I have faith in God. My faith/trust in God has given God the opportunity and allowed me to see God show his love and concern for my needs, desires, and overall well-being.

—Dawn Webb

7. Does your faith have an extraordinary sense of power or peace?

Yes, it does. I find that my sense of power and peace is far greater than many people I talk to, who fret over the state of the world, illnesses, or collapsing relationships. I do get sad sometimes, even anxious, but in the long run, I generally find peace, and I know that I am under the protective care and direction the Almighty God.

—Dr. Carol Cantu

Yes, I have faith in the Lord Jesus Christ. This gives me an extraordinary amount of power and peace in my spirit. My power comes because I know that I can all things through Christ because he strengthens me. He said that he would give me all the power over my enemy, I can walk among snakes and scorpions and crush them, and nothing will harm me. This means that I do not have to worry about those things that are up against me. They may look scary, may sound terrifying, seem dangerous, or look like something that can overtake me. However, having faith means to understand that nothing is too big for God to handle.

Knowing that God makes everything come out right for me because he loves me brings so much comfort. And when you are a child of God and you believe in him, he will move mountains, hardships, and evil antics out of our way. That's how special we are to him.

All we have to do is cast our cares on him because he cares for us. These things may sound just like words that people memorize, but it's much more to it than that. When one fully understands their meanings, that's when you have a true "aha" moment. You have to study it and read between the lines. When you begin to walk in what the Word says, that's when you feel the power of it. You have to have faith and only believe.

—Annece A. Hart

If I have faith in the idea that everything that happens in life is for the "good of all" no matter the outcome, it makes me feel at peace and empowered.

Sherrae' H.

I have peace and my Father in heaven shows me his power. Amazing things are then done.

—Shane H.

8. Have you felt the need to restore your faith? Why?

I have to say no. I think that going to church regularly and being connected to a faith support group [my church family] keeps my faith fed and renewed. Just like getting hungry or experiencing starvation tells you that you are lacking something or needing renewing, when you eat three balanced meals a day and follow general rules of nutrition, you seldom feel starvation. That is the same way with faith. Feeding myself regularly and staying connected to faith-renewing groups,

books, prayer, and regular means of inspiration, I
have not felt the need to restore my faith.

—Dr. Carol Cantu

I feel that since my faith is based on my
interactions with people and my world that my
faith is fluid in that I am gaining more in myself
and my ability to handle whatever comes my way.
I do wish to have my faith restored through positive purposeful relationships with God, Mother
Nature, and others. Having faith in the "greater
good" being an aim for the universe as a whole
is something I strive to replenish if it is attacked
and in decline because at the end of the day, I just
want to feel free, safe, and filled with positivity.

—Sherrae' H.

Yes! Sometimes I mess up with relationships, work, sin. I usually get a chance to seek
forgiveness and try again. I really appreciate the
Word of God. I usually see my mistakes being
revealed, but I then am showed a better way to
live.

—Shane H.

9. Has your faith been broken? If yes, how can you restore your
faith?

When my husband passed away, for a while,
I thought that my faith had been broken, but I
later realized it was not my faith that'd been broken; it was my joy that had been stolen. It still
has not been completely restored, but it is getting better. I realize that grieving takes about five
years. My husband passed away about three years
ago. The added sadness of losing my brother,

father-in-law, three sisters-in-law, and other relatives and friends in the last few years since my husband's death have slowed the process of joy restoration. But there are still many moments with family of joy, love, gladness, and fun. The birth of a new grandnephew, the many successes of family members, help to bring balance between sorrow and joy.

—Dr. Carol Cantu

Yes! Sometimes having faith in people of things can let you down. I have learned to forgive and to seek restorations. I have learned that God can make me over with the broken pieces, minded together by his Holy Spirit.

—Shane H.

No, not broken but evolved. My understanding and expectations have changed based on my experiences and my ability to understand how this world works. See answer to number 5 for more details.

—Sherrae' H.

10. Does your faith direct your daily behavior? Provide personal situations.

I believe so. I seriously try to please my Father in heaven daily. I'm not perfect at it and at times I feel bad when I don't do right. I then see the gift of forgiveness. This leaded me to the feeling of love.

—Shane H.

Allowing my faith to direct my daily behavior is my prayer each morning. I ask that everything I do every moment of the every day will be under the influence of the Holy Spirit and directed by faith. However, so much comes into our lives during the process of living that we get in the habit of just moving on, making decisions, completing jobs according to how we see it ought to be done, responding to questions with the first thing that comes to our minds. Stopping or slowing down enough to wait on the Lord is harder than we think. God made us intelligent beings with the power of choice. So we use our intelligence and we make decisions fast. Many times too fast. With each prayer I pray to start my day, I ask that the Lord will direct my path and slow me down to hear his voice as I go about my routines and as I encounter the challenges of life. I would not be honest if I said that my faith directs my daily behavior all of the time. But this is my goal. I am better than I used to be, but I am not yet where I want to be.

Recently, I stayed in a home that practiced very different religious rituals than I am used to. One of the men of the house asked me to read a paper that gave some insights into who they were and what religion they were. After I read the paper, the gentleman asked me what I thought of it. I did not want to offend him. I was the guest in his home. The people are loving, honest, and genuine God-fearing people. I did not want to lie and say, "It was nice." I felt that I was on the spot. But my faith (my following the Lord's lead) had me to say, "I will keep my thoughts to myself." I did not say it with attitude, arrogance, or malevolence. It was just a matter of fact response. I continued to smile whenever I saw the gentleman and he never brought up the matter again.

Another incident where I knew I was being led by faith was when I committed to having my grandson, Dymier, attend Pine Forge Academy. For me the cost was high, and I wanted to retire again so my finances would be less than usual. Somehow, his going to the school was not a matter of money, his not wanting to go, or what other naysayers were telling me. My faith was strong that Pine Forge was where he needed to be, and that finances would not stand in the way. Through a plan that was revealed to me, I took Dymier to register on the appointed date and was able to pay the entire bill on day one. I know that I was letting my faith dictate my behavior.

—Dr. Cantu

I have faith in the benefits of most Christian and Buddhist practices; therefore, I pray, meditate, and operate under a general "do no harm" policy unless it is to protect myself from harm. I rarely kill bugs if I can help it. I drink alcohol less than once a month and I have never treated sex or my relationships with others as a capitalist venture. I always want to operate from a sense of doing what is good for myself, others, and the world. I think of others most of the time, try to adhere to the Ten Commandments from the Bible, and attempt to follow the Eightfold Path of Buddhist philosophy, and I usually act out of love over personal gain.

—Sherrae' H.

11. Do you consider yourself a faithful servant? Why? Why not?

In my opinion, I consider myself to be a faithful servant. Am I at church every time the doors one? No. Am I involved in every commit-tee causing myself to be burnt out and living an unbalanced life? No. Am I perfect and never make mistakes? No. What I am doing is trying to live a life that is pleasing to God. After I asked Jesus to come into my life, change my way of thinking and doing, I have been determined to never let go of his hand or leading. It is not always easy because I am human and situations do not always deserve a "godly" response. Nonetheless, I push past that and have faith knowing that he is going to give me directions on how to respond. What I look forward to are times that I can be a blessing and help others if I feel old to do so. I try to be faithful when I do my absolute best to love everyone even though I may not like them or their actions.

I believe that I am faithful when I contin-ually read the Word of God and pray through-out my day, just talking to him about whatever is on my heart or in my mind. I am also becoming more faithful as I become involved in my church again in a way that I can help minister to people through song. I mean to have a life that in every-thing that I do exhibits God's presence. So yes, I consider myself a faithful servant.

—Annece H.

I try to be faithful. I focus on the little task before me and I usually finish the bigger task that way.

—Shane H.

This is a difficult question for a commit-ted Christian as I like to believe I am. I want to say yes because I want to believe I am and can give examples of things I have done. But at the same time, like the poem "Myself," I have to be true to myself. I see what others may never see. I know my thoughts. There are times when I may be faithful in doing a good work, but deep inside, I know I could have done more or I could have done better. There are times when I have given to a good cause, and I feel good about it. But then I ask, could I have given more? Did I give sacrificially? When it comes to my family and friends, I cannot think of anything I would not do or sacrifice, but am I the same way with those who I don't love as I love my family? That is another question. God says all are a part of his family, so therefore, I still should feel a family connection. But do I?

—Dr. Cantu

I try to be a faithful servant to what I believe is God's will, but I am imperfect and half of the time I am unsure exactly what that is. That changes according to the vast number of religions, but I do think they have the big important stuff in common such as their ethics and morals.

My father always said, "You know when you are doing wrong." I think he was right. I try to do what I think is right all the time. I do act from a place of love and try to positively protect and contribute to the betterment of people and the world. The opposite is acting out of God's service. I do my best and pray that that it is good enough. I aim for efficiency.

—Sherrae' H.

12. Do your external behaviors confirm and compliment your internal beliefs? Provide two examples.

> The answer to this question is very much the same as my answer to questions in 10. I would love to say yes. My external behaviors do confirm and compliment my internal beliefs. People who know me would probably say yes, but I have to ask the Lord to help me here. Am I a hypocrite? I don't have wings. I don't want to put my dirty laundry out there for all to see. But I have a way to go. I don't have any secret "big" sins. I am not a closet anything, but sin is sin and I am not ready for translation.
>
> —Dr. Cantu

> I believe so. I feel that I show my faith in God first by the way that I live and treat others. This helps me to give them my best love. Second, when I'm on a task that I've prayed about beforehand, I usually try to look past issues that arise. If God says more forward, I should almost expect adversity, but he makes the process successful for his glory.
>
> —Shane

> Yes, I do what I think is right according to my beliefs.
>
> —Sherrae' H.

13. Who in your lifetime has had a positive impact on your faith? Who? How?

> Man, where do I begin? I have a super-abundance of individuals who have had such a positive impact on my faith even to this day. I

am surrounded by people in my family, in my friend circle, and at my church that believe God and stand on his Word. We believe that his Word is true. However, the one individual who introduced me to the Lord, taught me about having faith, believing his Word, and understanding his principles was my mom.

Throughout my entire life up until her death, I watched her every move. Her life was based on prayer and having faith in God. My mother was a prayer warrior, so there were countless times that she was before the Lord about many situations that her or her family faced, calling out to him for numerous people that she knew and their circumstances, and she'd even be having conversations with the Lord about things yet to come. She never ceased from praying and in order for it to happen, she had to have faith.

One of her scriptures was "They that trust the Lord shall be at Mt. Zion, which cannot be moved, but abides forever." She had to stand firm in her faith for things to happen. Nothing could persuade her not to rust God. She knew that he was her strength and shield. She was human, and there were times she wanted to run in the opposite direction and not look back, but after much consideration, she chose to hold on to God's hand and have faith in his promises. Because of her perseverance, I watched as God worked on her behalf time after time. Many people saw it. That is probably why so many people were drawn to her because of her spirit and faith in God. I saw how what she prayed for came and is coming to past.

Even though she is no longer here, prayer that she prayed long before her death are still being honored because of her strong faith.

—Shane H.

There are too many people for me to name them all. I would have to start with my mother and then all of my siblings. There are other relatives, cousins, aunts and uncles, and in-laws; there are teachers, friends, and people I have admired and learned from even from afar. There are people I have read about and others whose lives I have watched on TV and in movies. Each one has added here a little and there a little. Some have modeled the principle of just be still and watch God work out the things that I have no idea about what to do. There are others who just always seem to know the right thing to do and to say without sweating and worrying. Some have prayed powerful prayers that had powerful results. Others have just lived such amazingly good lives that I could not help but see faith in action. I cannot name just one. And if I get started on naming just a few, I would not be able to stop.

—Dr. Cantu

My parents raised me in a Christian-based home environment, and they sent me to Christian schools, so it has all had an effect. My grandmother and mother used to read the Bible with me as a child, and they took me to church, so I guess being in a family that adheres to a religion made me a bit religious. As it relates to religion, you pretty much adopt that to which you are exposed. I was exposed to a lot compared to most people before I was old enough to drive. I went to a Quaker high school where I studied the Bible for about a year, life philosophies, and world religions for about year and that included Buddhism. I came to appreciate Buddhist philosophy because it just made sense to me. I think all of my family members are in some form Christian or Muslim, etc. Whether or not they practice in accordance to other people's guidelines is possibly another story. Watching how each of my family members has dealt with their wins and losses has positively affected my faith in the goodness of God, most religions and my abilities to survive and thrive in this world if I am faithful to what I believe to be right.

—Sherrae' H.

Parents. When I see them pray and push through hard times by faith. My wife: she is a prayer warrior. She does a great job at serving other and power pack praying. Her prayers get answers.

—Shane H.

14. Can faith evoke miracles? Explain.

(See stories in the book On Your Way, 28–30)

My niece Marilyn had a dilemma, she needed to work; she also needed to be in school full time, order to be covered by my insurance. Juggling her work schedule and her school schedule proved to be an impossibility, unless she took a court on Saturday_ a conflict with her religious conviction of observing Saturday as the Sabbath.

She refrained from all work and school obligations, to rest and reflect on all spiritual things.

Marilyn saw no way out of this dilemma. I had no advice for her, either. So, I simply told her that," God would work this one out. Just stand still and see how he does it. And when He does, acknowledge His power, His wisdom, and His love.

In the morning after prayer, we both decided to make some telephone calls. I would call the insurance company to check on the status on both Marilyn and Mia, who were both in colleges, and she would see if there was a possibility for purses other than Saturday, that did to conflate with her work schedule. She would also see if her work schedule could be adjusted. She had done all this investigating before, but she would give it one more try.

Marilyn's results were the same as always. However, something unusual happened when I called the insurance company. I was prepared to report that both girls were in college again, but that Marilyn was having difficulty arranging her schedule, to carry a full load. I knew that the answer to my next question would be no, but I asked it anyhow: Are there any exceptions to the rule of having to take a full course load to be covered by insurance? To my surprise, I was not allowed to ask the question. The agent informed me, that everything with Marilyn was ok. She asked me few questions about Mia. I answered her and again attempted to turn the conversation to Marilyn. She informed me again, that there was no problem with Marilyn. She was covered by the insurance and everything with her was fine. This agent was beginning to sound upset with me for trying to persist in discussing Marilyn's situation She refused to allow me to talk.

After several unsuccessful attempts, I humbly and thankfully ended the conversation It was settled. Marilyn was covered by the insurance without taking the course on Saturday. When I Tod Marilyn the news, at the end of the day, we rejoiced. We gave God the glory, and the honor for being who He is and for handling in such a simple and easy way, what to us was Red Sea experience. We marveled at how God operates.

How can anyone think that the Christian life is dull? It is exciting and amazing when you stand still and see for yourself the salvation of the Lord in your life. (Dr. Cantu)

I believe that faith can evoke miracles. As a matter of fact, I know that this absolutely true. Our son was born twenty-seven-week premature. He was 1 lb. 13 oz. Our little guy came into the old fighter and fight is what he did. He definitely was not in it alone. Our faith went into overdrive. In spite of preparing us for the worse, just in case something went wrong, we kept our eyes on God our son's life depended on to. Regardless of the oxygen tanks, the tubes, the shots, the infections, the jaundice, other babies gravely sick around him, we trusted the God would make everything come out right for us. Many people were kept at bay and we kept our focus on God's promises. Amazingly, we did not have a feeling that anything was going to go wrong. We looked at it as the baby case really early. He has to fight and we just have to do what has to be done so that he can come home as soon as possible. We had such a peace during this time, it blew people's minds. Because of our faith, God kept giving us signs that he had everything under control. For example our son was in the "Dove" room. In the Bible the dove represents the Holy Spirit and he gave us a sense of peace. He was given bed 12, which is a perfect number that symbolized God's power and authority. So we knew by faith that God was governing this situation.

Fast forward: After our long hospital stay, we were finally able to take our son home. We were thinking, "Okay, baby, now we have to ween you off these oxygen tanks and you'll be good to go." We watched as he began to grow. He got tired of the oxygen and been to breathe on his own. YES! But as monthly milestones would come, we noticed he was not fully developing as each day passed by. The baby would be able to do many things, but major marks like sitting up crawling, standing, and walking were being missed. Come to find out he had a condition called spastic diplegia, which is a form of cerebral palsy that affected his leg and ankle cord's spasticity. This new venture led to many years of types of therapies, many procedures, a ton of weekly doctor appointments, and numerous assistive devices for walking. It was extremely emotional times, but what kept us motivated was focusing on God as he improved our son's quality of life.

We had to have faith and believe that just like his Word says, "But He was wounded for our transgressions, bruised for our iniquities, the chastisement of our peace was upon him and with His stripes we are healed." We had to believe that God's Word is true. We could not be persuaded any other way by looking at the negative of what was going on. Yes, we were exhausted. Yes, we felt weary at times. Yes, we were concerned about how our son was going to be able to cope with what he was dealing with. We are parents. Nonetheless, we never gave up believing and *never* let our son quit.

He never liked to be left behind anyway, so he learned being on his tiptoes to his advantage. His feet were never flat on the floor. He had never felt a surface with his feet. We had to do something. This was going to get painful as he grew because he was eventually going to gain more weight. We knew deep down our hearts that our son was going to be healed of this. We were not satisfied with all of the things we had to put him through time after time, just to back at square one.

So in 2008, my husband and I said, "Enough is enough." We prayed for specific instructions concerning the route we should take concerning our son's medical treatment.

Our faith was in overdrive. Doctors were saying there were limited ways to deal with his condition, that in our opinion were futile. It felt like they were just placing a Band-Aid over a cut instead of dealing with true issue.

So we sought God, researched more on our son's diagnosis and available treatments, prayed, and fasted. After a while, God started opening doors and allowing people that were chosen to help us during this time to cross our path, confirming that we are on the right track.

To catapult to the end of this segment, we ended up communicating with this doctor and his associate, all the way in St. Louis, Missouri, who was the top doctor out of three in the country. He performs a very unique surgery; that was just what our son needed. God had given this doctor the wisdom and the ability to attack our son's problem at the root.

It was a very serious surgery, but our faith in God moved mountains. He is so awesome. He is so awesome. He never falls short of his promises, and He cannot lie. That was when our child was eight years old.

Today he is thirteen years old, walking flat footed (a little too much), playing basketball, is an awesome drummer, and loves ushering in church. This is the same baby that could not sit up, crawl, stand, or walk. Having faith, trusting in God's Word, and listening to him clearly did that.

Yes, the doctors may have performed the surgeries, but God is the one that gave them the knowledge and ability to do it. Trust in the Lord with all your heart and lean not on thine own understanding. In all ways acknowledge Him and He hall direct you path (Bible V).

—Annece H.

Yes, I recently had a stomach issue for several weeks that would not go away. We went to a weekly church meeting in Chester. While there my pastor asked if anyone wants prayer. I thought, "Yes, for my stomach." He prayed for me and two days later I felt back to my normal self after several weeks. I went to the doctor, took meds; nothing was working. The prayer made the difference.

I believe in miracles, so I hope so. I think this entire experience of people and the planets, etc. is a miracle. Life itself is a miracle outside of my own understanding. I don't know that faith evokes miracles, meaning it creates them but I do believe it provides opportunities and environments for them to occur. Faith is like the womb where a miracle can come into being, a safe space for the growth and birth of possibilities. Things that people believe are impossible are only made possible through someone first having faith that just maybe something different could happen. For example, when people come back to full functionality from comas, it is someone's faith that kept that person on life, supportive long enough for the needed healing to take place which would eventually lead to what no one knew would be a full recovery. It is safe to say that without faith, fewer miraculous events would have been experienced for sure. Faith provides people with the will and power to give something a try and sometimes that try becomes a win and that win...a miracle.

—Sherrae' L. Hartie

15. Are you currently suffering with a self-to-self conflict? Explain.

Love, patience, faithfulness, self-control, kindness, goodness, and gentleness are the fruit of the spirit. In the Bible, they are considered together. If one is missing, the other eight must also, according to me, be compromised. So yes, I struggle. But I know that I am still grieving, and grief takes at least five years to subside. So I do what I can, I read what is available, I attend worship services, I try to serve others. And I pray that my faith will be strengthened and my joy made complete.

—Dr. Cantu

I deal with self-conflict constantly, but I use my morals, my ethics, and my desire to do what is right to help me determine the best thing for me to do in the end. Sometimes, I ask for spiritual guidance or help. I have faith that I am doing my best, but I haven't always had the best outcomes in every situation. This has led me to not always have the greatest faith that a situation or decision will benefit me most, but I pray and I meditate and I hope my identified resolution to a conflict leads me to the results I long to achieve.

—Sherrae' H.

Yes, my humanity gets in the way of what I feel my Father in heaven wants for me to do. I sometimes feel lead to pray for someone; to simply share Christ with someone or move in a new direction in life and I get nervous. I start to doubt or second-guess the things I know is happening.

—Shane H.

16. Do you have a self-to-others issue? How will you address the situation?

I am not aware of this kind of issue in my life. If there is someone who has an issue with me, I do hope they make it known so that I can do what is necessary to resolve it. I have had these issues in the past, but not now. Spiritual maturity and the passing of time have brought closure to many of the old problems and the old mindset. I have learned that I do not have to give every thought a verbal expression. I have learned to appreciate others' points of view. I have become content with allowing others to be wrong, and I don't have to always be right myself.

—Dr. Cantu

If I do I usually pray and ask my Father in heaven how to resolve the issue. Sometimes he fixes it; other times I'm lead to peacefully confront the person. This could be a little nerving, but it usually works out well.

—Shane H.

Sometimes, I have conflicts with people close to me who don't want to know or contend with facts and I struggle with knowing when to and when not to share too much of an observation with them if we are in a personal relationship, family or friends. It's in my nature to want to help. I simply feel that sometimes I get punished for my responses. When working as a coach or a counselor, there are different boundaries and expectations that come with conversing. People don't take my opinion personally because they know it's coming from a learned perspective, but when I am dealing with friends or family, it's different. Because of the power, weight, or delivery of my questions or analysis, sometimes my professional skills cause me personal conflicts. Turning it off can be a challenge when you hear someone ask for help or you see people struggling who you like, love, or care about, but I realized not everyone is prepared for what's about to come out of my mouth, and the things that seem so obvious to me are not always that way for them. I want to be of assistance, keep the peace, and not have to walk on eggshells around people, but that's not always a possibility. Sometimes, I'm going to say

things or give answers and they don't like it. It
has caused conflict when I touch exposed nerves
people have forgotten were even there. It's never
my intention to hurt feelings.

—Sherrae' H.

17. Reflections: What have you internalized from this faith journey?
(Have you discovered anything about your faith journey as a
result of answering questions 16? If so, what?)

Looking back on these various times in my
life, one thing stands true. God is faithful to us.
If he said that he will do it, look for it to come
to past. "So is my word that goes out from my
mouth, it will not return to me empty, but will
accomplish what I desire and achieve the purpose
for which I have sent it."

All we have to do is speak his word back
to him, trust, and have faith in his promises. I
am thankful to him for never having me nor for-
saking me. Even those times when I did or do
not deserve his love and compassion, he still loves
me. Let me make this clear… If anyone is having
a difficult time deciding to have faith in God, do
not hesitate. It is the best decision you will ever
make. My world has been tremendously blessed
because of his presence in my life.

—Annece H.

This opportunity to evaluate and reflect has
been an amazing experience for me. Writing all
of this down, I have come to realize that what
I thought was a loss of faith was not. It was a
loss of joy that is a natural part of grief. This
journey has increased my faith to know for sure
that the joy will be restored and that God will

bring it back multifold as he has already started the process. This restoration has come a lot from Dr. Faith and Sherrae' and from my late brother Allen. It is also coming through my sister-in-law, Rissie, who is on a faith walk of her own. And she has lovingly included me on her walk, which is bringing back joy. My cousin Dwight wrote a note that said that when Rissie hits the home run in her faith journey fighting cancer, she will bring us all into home plate. That is happening to me. So thank you, Dr. Faith, for what you are doing. It has been a tremendous blessing for me. And the blessings are just beginning.

—Dr. Cantu

As a result of answering these questions, I have discovered my personal definition of what a miracle is to me. I realize that having faith in the possibilities of what you want to happen actually happening is a key component to miracles having a chance to manifest. So it reinforces what I've learned from my father, that luck is when preparation meets opportunity, and what I've learned from my mother that my faith, your faith, our faith truly, without a doubt, changes everything.

—Sherrae' H.

I have internalized that the Lord is truly real and he loves me. It is best to move close to him.

—Shane H.

Part 2

Your Faith

Contributors
Annece Adamson-Hart, educator
Dr. Carol Cantu, educator, author
Sherrae' L. Hartie, educator, therapist
Marilyn S. Jamal, educator, So. Jersey Teen Shop director
Dawn Webb, social worker
Rev. Shane Hartie, pastor, educator, realtor

Faith Seed

Faith of a mustard seed is what we hold dear
In life we suffer
In life we confront and overcome challenges
That contain enormous moments of fear
In life we often replicate sins and wins
But the faith of a mustard seed
Usually assures us a rebound and a positive mend

In life we celebrate
In life we calculate
In our lives we choose to thrive and survive
The unpredictable life's journey and our fate

The tiny little mustard seed can and will grow
If we increase our spirituality by devouring God's word
And live the life in His light and the seed
Will absolutely glow and grow

Your faith seed is yours to care for
It will be there for you every time
If you try to live His word
And always seek his grace and mercy more.

Hartie's   Webb's

Part 3

Our Faith

Our Faith

This faith journey has served me in several important, life-changing ways. As noted in the beginning of this book, Allen L. Hartie, my deceased husband, had recently gone on to glory. My forty-seven-year marriage represented my entire adult life. The transformation from married to single has been very alarming. I have matured emotionally, physically, and psychologically over the duration of our marriage.

Changes occurred in the both of us during the nearly five decades of togetherness. Notedly, we fell in and out of love numerous times but never stopped loving each other. For better or worse, we plowed through all the "stuff!" The marriage taught me that God rules. God ordered our steps to maintain this special partnership. This union was sustained through all matters of evil. God provided each of us with the insight and determination to make it, the relationship righteous in His sight. Only God was responsible for the success we experienced.

Each of us had faith and trust in the Lord. We both gave him the credit and the praise for all he delivered in our lives. This faith journey reminded me of all God's grace and mercy. I will attempt to give this phase of my life to the honor and glory of the Lord Jesus Christ.

I am writing more inspirational works to enlighten, encourage, and inspire others to acknowledge through thought, word, and deeds the concept of "God's power!"

It has been revealed to me as I talked to contributors and read their shared faith experiences in part 2 of this book that all of the people in the world are exposed to and impacted by faith. A multitude of stories are yet to be told, but we all have some.

The ideologies, trust, confidence, beliefs, and conviction that are internalized by us all during maturation evoke the faith behaviors we practice in life situations. Our lives are guided by these five pillars of faith, regardless as to the formal, orthodox or unorthodox religion we subscribe to in our spiritual practice daily.

In conclusion, this faith journey has proven insightful. The self-introspection and reflection have been enlightening and enriching to my soul, heart, and mind.

I hope and pray the readers will strongly reflect and encourage on the self-to-self experience. Use it each day to evoke positive and purposeful decisions. Also use the five pillars of your faith to conscientiously and successfully use the self-to-others model, to improve, embrace, and enhance your professional and personal relationships with others.

Faith in *your* Higher Power is the spiritual force of *your* life!

Walk in *your* faith!

As I reflect the self to self and the self to others principle, I realize that many of us are very comfortable, competent, and confident when making decisions or implementing paradigm shifts impacting self. We often can make determinations that effect our own lives without much input from others. Some people's faith in self and God, create an inner wiring allowing them to be more apt to depend on their own decision-making skills, even though self to self decisions can be extremely, demoralizing, and hurtful. But for many it is rewarding, satisfying, and purposeful. Your faith and self confidence can make all the difference in your flow in this world. Considering relationships, jobs, transitions, divorce, and other life changing choices is a large part of this thing called life.

As we revisit the the self to others model, it is apparent through the eyes of the world that people need people, the human race seeks the acceptance, understanding, acquiescence, and approval of mankind. The degree to which these factors are sought vary, upon the individual internal wiring. Our internal network the heart, mind, body, and soul all inadvertently respond to human reactions to us. The levels of human need vary pending the inner self network. Self to others situations are inevitably influenced and shaded by the "Need" factor, you possess.

Including, one, two, or more individuals in the self to others experience can ultimately persuade your choice(s) of action(s) and/or change your final decision(s).

Depending upon your inner wiring, your personal flow, the self to self vs the self o others experience model will most definitely add or subtract from the smooth flow of your life.

Part 4

Poetry Nook

Faith and Me

My faith guides me
My faith sustains me
My faith inspires me
My faith enlightens me
And builds in me, righteousness

My faith is based on these five pillars:
Ideologies
Trust
Belief
Confidence
And Conviction

My faith is powerful
My faith propels
And protects me

My faith is my life's map to righteousness

Awaken Faith

God opens your eyes each and every day
We lunge with some enthusiasm into work and or play
Our heavenly Father lifts up our spirits
And sometimes mankind brings them down

We trust and believe God's power
Will meticulously direct our steps
In the paths of righteousness and
Mold our spirituality to create
Positive experiences leading to acts
Of fruitfulness, goodness, and kindness

Awaken we are
to the omnipotence
and majesty
of His works
We constantly strive
to obtain His approval
We live our daily lives
hoping and praying
That the Lord will be satisfied
With our intentions
With our interactions
And
With our spiritual dedication

Jesus

Jesus, Jesus, Jesus
He is the ultimate spiritual man
The Alpha and the Omega
The beginning and the end

Jesus rules the world
And manages the universe's magical evolution
With his mighty, masterful, meaningful plan
Around the sun
The earth spins in his mighty hand

Jesus keeps the universe
flowing
Smoothly and methodically
spinning
On its natural axis
Riveting
As his earthly children
honor his words in their practice
to live a Christ-like life
They faithfully strive

Signs of 2020

Extreme and critical situations all over the world
Witnessed by men, women, boys and girls
Nearly everywhere you look
Devastation, insecurity, Conflict, and Confusion Exist
Putting all human beings and our own sweet Democracy at-risk
Are severe signs of 2020

Feeling of being, shaken, taken, and awaken
to a frightening new world
Signs of 2020
Thousands of people are dying, crying, and feel
like their flying into a immovable force
A sign of 2020
Feeling scared, tired, pained, and strained
Signs of 2020

Chaos, struggle, crisis, and hurt,
Wearing face masks, social-distancing, and the
frequent washing hands to kill germs and dirt
Signs of 2020

Challenging your convictions and faith in mankind
A sign of 2020
Forcing your tolerance to
A point of sheer intensity
Signs of 2020

Shortage of food, ppe's, and patience, shortage of jobs and money
Cause people to fret and scurry
Encouraging leadership to make life more livable and safe
Empowering our society not to give up or and not to worry
Signs of 2020

Extreme times, needing extraordinary measures
To quell the world of global protests and
mitigate the systemic racial tensions
Lives are deemed expendable, so unlike
many other worldly treasures
Signs of 2020

The pandemic, corona virus, or covid-19
You choose the name
It is all the same
Invisible killer of men, women, and children of all ages
Have been, will be victims of the silent killer strain
That has taken the world by storm and caused
immense and unforgettable pain
Signs 0f 2020

Your faith and trust in God are called upon more often than
not, for peace of mind, comfort, and encouraging thoughts
Signs of 2020

Needing love, hope, and kindness in haunting times like these
Signs of 2020

You know, we have some Corrupted Politicians, Immigration
situations, Environmental Conditions, Impeachment
moments, Economic Depression and Voter Suppression,
Compounded with Corona have created and nurtured
Extreme signs of a frayed, frightening, and
frustrating 2020 Depression
Signs of 2020

Our students have been out of school since March
Remote/Virtual learning is in action
But, you know, Many of the students are
not getting much satisfaction
There is no definite time to restart brick mortar
So our students' and their families, are
in a state of complete disorder
Signs of 2020

Everyday essential workers are put to the test

They work, and work for patients and all of us
And get very little rest, they fear for their
lives and there families too
Treacherous Pandemic, you make this horrible, deadly,
Life oh, so true
Signs of 2020

SCJ, NOTORIOUS RBG. Congressmen J. E. Clyburn,
John Lewis, VP Joe Biden, Senator Kamala Harris, Joy Reid,
Corey Booker and Atlanta's Mayor, Keisha Lance Bottoms
Just to name a few, made cultural history, tis true
Signs of 2020

Victims, George Floyd, Ahmaud A., Eric
G., MIchael B., and Breonna T.
Oh..., All gone too soon!
Black Lives Matter Too!
Signs of 2020

Clap, Clap!! to all the 2020 Graduates, as they hurl their
caps to the sky, and declare 2020 an absolute win
Though they took numerous hard hits on the shin!
No class trip, No Senior Day, No Senior Prom,
No traditional Commencement Exercise

Yet, these 2020 Graduates, still stand tall and
continue to soar and achieve more and more!

Still they Rise!
Signs of 2020

History proves this too shall pass, as brilliant scientist
feverishly are working at finding a vaccine
That will cure our infected land of Covid-19
A sign of 2020

Our country is experiencing grand transformation
Glass ceilings are being broken everyday
As the country elects Joe Biden for president
And Kamala Harris , first woman, and further noted, first
Black/Asian woman to our nation's office of Vice President
Signs of 2020

We will overcome and continue living life as we do
And 2020 will be remembered
As a time of crisis, death, courage, evolution, and virtue

A tumultuous, transformational, and
transitional time called 2020
Forever in our minds
Signs of 2020
Signs of 2020
Signs of 2020

Dr. Faith E. Hartie 8/8/20

THANK YOU, to all persons that contributed in any way to the birth of this book, Dr. Faith on Faith, The Realties. Special Thanks to my Educational Mentors:

Dr. Mary Arnold Frazier, Dr. Wilma Farmer, Michael P. Hailey, Dorothy W. Wyatt, and Calvin Gunning. Your mentorships assisted me in my professional development and I truly evolved into the educational administrator I always sought to become! Thank You All. You were truly my village!!!

Faith Notes for Thought

Faith Notes for Thought

Faith Notes for Thought

_____

_____

_____

_____

_____

_____

_____

_____

_____

_____

_____

_____

_____

Faith Notes for Thought

_____

_____

_____

_____

_____

_____

_____

_____

_____

_____

_____

_____

_____

_____

_____

_____

_____

Bibliography

- God's Little Devotional Book for Women, 1996 by Honor Book Inc., PO Bx. 55388 in Tulsa Oklahoma.
- On Your Way, 2001 by Carol Cantu, Vantage Press, Inc. 516 W. 34th St, NY, NY.
- Prayers for a Woman of Faith, 1998, by New Life Clinics

About the Author

Faith E. Hartie, EDd, was born in 1948 to parents Betty L. and Malachai C. Adamson. She was married to Allen L. Hartie for forty-seven years, ending upon his death in 2018. They were blessed with one daughter, Sherrae' L. Hartie. Dr. Faith E. Hartie was an educator for forty-two years, serving the Camden City School District. Her educational journey was amazing and memorable, having serviced thousands of youth, parents, and colleagues. She was honored as Teacher of the Year at the Lanning Square School. Dr. Hartie served as a classroom teacher, English teacher, writing teacher, teacher mentor, curriculum supervisor, principal, and director of secondary curriculum and instruction. Dr. Hartie also worked for the Philadelphia Department of Recreation from age fourteen to approximately twenty-five years old. Starting as a summer camp counselor and rising to an assistant recreation leader(ARL). During her years as an ARL, she found a passion for fashion through the city's Model Teen Program for youth. She later opened her own modeling agency, CEO of Faith Hartie's Model, Inc. During this era of her life, she directed the models in the agency to perform local fashion shows and extravaganzas. She connected to local fashion boutiques and department stores for runway and print work. She always enjoyed writing.

She wrote plays for the youth at recreation centers and schools where she was employed. In 2018, she was inspired to write this book on *faith*. It reveals some intimate *faith* experiences had by herself and six others. Dr. Hartie hopes to encourage, empower, and inspire the readers to embrace life's challenges with positivity, determination, and faith. Dr. Hartie is a lifetime member of the AME Union Church, a golden member of Delta Sigma Theta Inc. Sorority, and a member of National Sorority of Phi Delta Kappa.

rmation can be obtained
esting.com
JSA
20721
1B/12